Publisher:

The Motivational Club (Pty) Ltd
4 De Beer Street
Braamfontein
Johannesburg
2001
Republic of South Africa

Tel: +27 (0) 11 046 9394
E-mail: publish@motivationalclub.co.za
Website: www.motivationalclub.co.za

Author's Contacts:

Facebook: Lethabokenedy Morwatshehla
Twitter: @lethabokenedy
Instagram: @Lethabokenedy Morwatshehla
E-mail: Lethabokenedylethabo@gmail.com
WhatsApp: +27 (0) 72 798 4062

ISBN 978-0-620-80452-3

GENUINE DREAM

<<<Contents>>>

Acknowledgements

To my parents who helped me save money to publish this book, they showed me love and the support I needed in the process of writing this book; to my sister Dikeledi who believed in me when I told her about my dream of writing a book, she is the one who encouraged me when I felt discouraged most times. To my former primary school teachers who took their times to impart me with basic knowledge and to my former high school teachers who trained me to be useful in life. Many thanks also to everyone who helped me publish this book.

To all my Whatsapp and Facebook Friends who gave me supports, thanks I appreciate them for their kindness. Thanks to my childhood friends and to my community. Finally I appreciate everyone who is busy reading this book. Thank you all, you are the best, without you guys I am not complete, you are all playing an important role in my life, no words can explain how favoured I am to have you guys. Thank you all!

Lethabo kenedy Morwatshehla

Preface

This book consists of fundamental strategies that will enable one to be certain about his or her dream and it's a tool that can change ones' perspectives and belief about life. It touches every aspects of a dreamer in order to help the dreamer fulfil his or her dream. It aligns you with your dream. It will help you understand the difference between a good and a great dream, since many people are confused about what they want in life, this book will help them figure out what they want in life. This book is written in order to equip the unequipped in every aspect of their lives.

This book will make you a fanatic of your own dream. It always seems to be hard to reach your dream without guidance, so this book will direct you to your designated place, this book is for those who are willing to take risks in order to reach their dreams. As a matter of fact you are the right person to read this book, because it is not too late to reach your dream, I believe that your dream was waiting for this book in order to be activated, this book does not only activate your dream, it will accelerate your dream and will provoke you to reach your dream without any doubts. For as long as you are holding this weapon in your hand you cannot fail to reach your dream. There are some significant improvements that will take place in your life after reading this piece of writing. Never give up until you reach it. This book will give you an idea of what your dream requires in order to be reached. God gave you the ability to dream, that is why this book was specially written for you to use it in order to provoke your dreaming ability. God is there to sustain in your journey of reaching your dream. God has favoured you with his grace, which will also sustain you. You are a legend and every sentence of this book will have an impact in your life and dream. Don't stop dreaming.

Most importantly don't stop trying when you fail, remember you cannot fail when you are not doing anything, it means that when you fail you are on the right path that leads to your dream; failing is a sign of being on the right path.

Recently I discovered that most people have dreams, but their dreams do not seem genuine and what makes a genuine dream is the faith you have. Never stop dreaming, even the trees never stops producing leaves and fruits, but only a dead tree can stop producing, and because you are not dead continue working on your dream.

CHAPTER 1

<u>*Process that leads to your dream*</u>

We accompanied our dreams here on earth so that they may have a great impact in our generation, but it is up to us to usher our dreams and sweat for them, so that we may fulfil them.

Everyone was born for a reason, no one was born without a purpose. We have a way of believing in our dreams and specific ways of reaching our dreams in order to make them real. Dreams can be crushed but there is a way to resurrect them. I believe that every dream that seems to be dead can come back to life and fulfil its purpose .Don't let anything destruct you when aiming to reach your dream. Have a dream.

Once upon a time there was a little frog in the desert, the frog was not aware that it had a dream, until it associated itself with a wrong crowd. Sometimes being associated with wrong people might help you discover your dream, because they are not going to feel pity for you, sometimes we need wrong people in our lives in order to help us discover our dreams, Not always but sometimes; the more they don't feel pity for you that's the more you will realise that you don't belong in their crowd, you will then set yourself apart from them and try to discover your destiny and dream. Sometimes being involved in a wrong crowd might give you an opportunity to realise that you need to stand on your own.

Some of us can discover our dreams in the absence of wrong people, it's not compulsory to be associated with the wrong crowd, but it's compulsory to stand on your own when you have a dream.

This small frog was alone in the desert, which was extremely dry, than other deserts. The frog survived by the small stream and the stream was not an active one; even the frog knew that one day the stream will run dry, there was no rain during that time as it was spring season. It was not easy for the frog to cope in the desert, because of its present difficulties. The difficulties of the frog took place at the right time in order to prepare the frog for where it was going.

To every thing there is a season. Things happen for a reason, everything that happened in your life was not a mistake, things that happened in your life were meant to help you to be here today. I often hear people say that "its not your problem to be born poor, but it's your problem to die poor" were you born poor? If you were born poor you were not supposed to possess the qualities you have. Everyone was born wealthy. You must stop cursing your background, say: **I was born to create and I can do all things.** Nobody was born poor.

There are many people who survive by making use of their abilities, they make money in order to buy food for the day, but this is not enough because sometimes they can spend the whole day without making money. We all need more than one stream of income in our lives so that we don't struggle. I believe that everyone could be wealthy by reaching his dream. Our dreams can help us stop struggle.

Sometimes we find ourselves being in the desert where we only have one source of income of which we cannot rely on for the rest of our lives. We find that our lives are in danger, because of the storms that shakes us when we try to stand up. The Strom can shake the tree and even uproot the tree, but it's up to the tree to allow the Strom to uproot it, if the roots of the tree are not strong, then the storm will a have a chance to uproot the tree. Don't allow the storm to uproot you.

Sometimes we get discouraged and start thinking that our potentials are limited, that is why we depend on one thing for a long time, reason being is that we are not living our DREAM. Sometimes it's not easy to depend on something which is dysfunctional, because we also end up being dysfunctional, there are many things we can do in life in order to have many streams of income. Our dream is one element, which has the ability to create many streams of income for us; Hence where there is a dream, there is perfection and there is liberty. Our dream has ways of opening more doors for us.

The frog felt lonely in the desert, it ended up losing hope that one day it could have friends and more sources of water where it can stay and the streams which it can rely on to survive, because the current situation was tough. The frog was experiencing horrific days. One day the frog was looking at the sky and said "how can you forsake me" then its tears overflowed and started pleading. The frog thought that it came to the world to do nothing because it had no faith during that time. The place where the frog could find an active stream was about 100 metres away from where it was, but the frog told itself that it's over with it.

The frog developed doubt and remember that doubt have the potency to disqualify anyone from reaching their destination; hence do not develop doubt as you pursue your dream, learn to always be courageous.
You should never doubt your dreams. They can be tangible, that's why you should be courageous, for nothing can come true in the absence of courage. Courage is what makes you believe, it gives you access to face anything of any magnitude in life. Know that without courage defeat is inevitable. You cannot achieve that golden dream without courage. Many tried but they failed, courage is what gives you the idea of pushing, even if the situation does not allow you to.

Don't try to achieve your dream in the absence of courage. You will try but you will never see the benefits of trying, be courageous. The golden dream consists of courage that is in the heart of a dreamer.

When you are a human being you should understand that you will encounter inevitable challenges. You must face those challenges in order to make you stronger; you must endure the pain of being in difficult challenges so that when better days come you will enjoy them. Don't blame anyone when you go through hell, challenges will not be the same as your brother's or sister's. Endure the pains.

Not everything in life will come easy, you may have potential but potential does not turn to greatness it requires hard work, dedication, discipline. Don't give up on your dreams, work for your dreams and don't allow the process to stop you from going where you want to be. There is a process for everything in life, the process might take long or might not be long. Allow the process to prepare you for where you are going, don't blame your process, be grateful and know that your process is equipping you.

Your home is where you are going, your dream is your home, so don't allow anything to *impede* you from going home, there is no other home for you. When you reach your dreams, you will experience Joy in your life. Where there is no Joy there is no home, home is a place of Joy not of happiness. Happiness is temporary; don't allow happiness to be the reason for not going home. Go home, reach your dreams and don't be lost forever, don't be paralyzed mentally. Reach your dreams and experience the real Joy of life.

One day the frog decided to move around the desert to look for another stream, the frog was doubting that it could find any.

When the frog was busy moving around the desert it decided to change its thoughts. The frog decided to have positive thoughts, the frog realised that only positive thoughts could turn things around and change its current situation for the better.

The frog realised that the only way to conquer challenges, is the way one sees things and start to see things differently.
At the moment that the frog started having positive thoughts, that's when it started having a vision for the future. When you have negative thoughts its impossible to have a great vision for the future. Thoughts creates the future and the ideas of the future creates vision and vision brings strength to help you run the race of life.
Thinking positively starts when one knows how to have a positive thought pattern. When one has a good thought pattern its easy for them to think positively and know how to bring his thoughts into life.

The frog moved around the dessert, hoping to find an active stream, but there was only one stream in the desert which was no longer active. While the frog was moving around, the frog found a dead ant in the desert. The frog was shocked and surprised, the frog told it self that, this place is too dangerous, because some insects in the area were dying. The frog was not used to the environment though. While it was moving around, it wondered about its own survival, while other animals are dying.

The frog believed that maybe its strength and the strength of other animals are not the same and does not have the same power. When one realises that his or her abilities can activate things that people are not able to activate, it is then that one starts to believe that life is the same, but the abilities and attitudes are **not the same, they** differ. Never compare your strength with someone's strength, your strength is adequate for you.

Demonstrating your strength must be coupled with knowing your abilities. You cannot have strength in the absence of your abilities.

As a dreamer you need to understand that you can find yourself in an environment which you are not used to. You have to pass where you don't belong for the preparation of your future, So that you could be strong in the future for the sake of your success. Behind every success there is a painful struggle. You need to be focused when you meet some challenges which are too dangerous for you in order for you to overcome them. You need to understand that your challenges do not determine your future.
You need to understand that your future revolves around your thoughts. Sometimes we make a mistake and often think that our thoughts are just temporary. We are who we are today, because of our previous thoughts. We have to learn that, what we think we become and what we ignore becomes our enemy.

The frog was wondering why some animals are dying, while it was the only one surviving in a place where many other animals were dying, the frog then started to realise that there is something about it-self. The frog started to rehabilitate its strength and preparing for the worse that could come along its way. The frog was prepared to face further difficult challenges. The frog told itself that it could conquer everything that could come along its way, then it started to realise that sometimes it's not easy to live life.

While the frog was rehabilitating its strength, a small insect passed by pushing a small round ball. The frog was looking at the small insect, then saw another small ball on the side where the insect was coming from, it then went there to take the ball and do the same as the insect. The frog was so excited to push the small round ball; the reason why it was excited is because it was easy to push the small round ball in the dessert.

CHAPTER 1

The frog loved pushing the ball, just to make time to go on, but the frog was not passionate about it. But the frog decided to follow the decisions of other animals.

The frog never took the decision to push the ball by itself, but was influenced by the insect in order to please them. The insect was really pleased seeing other animals enjoy doing what it does on a daily basis to survive. The insect thought that the frog loved pushing things around whilst the frog was just doing it to please the insect, because the frog knew that it does not belong in that environment. The frog started having some skills of pushing those small round balls and the insect was excited.

The insect thought that the frog will never go where it came from, it will spend the rest of its life in the desert, the frog knew that one day there could be a possibility for it to go back home where it came from.

The frog started taking orders from the insect in order to please it. The frog knew very well that one day it will find it self in an active stream. The frog wanted to have offsprings but its situation didn't allow it to do so, but the frog knew very well that if it get a chance to be in water for two days, its desire will come to pass and be fulfilled. "Sometimes things do not come easily, but one needs dedication and patience.

I would have been far if I had faith years ago, but I doubted my faith, hence I was stuck in life. "The decision I took few weeks back made my life miserable" the frog said. Sometimes in life when you try to do an introspection there are some people who will come in your life and do it for you. They will take decisions on your behalf, they will make sure that you do what pleases them. They will try by all mean to control you; as a matter of fact they just don't want you to do things by yourself.

The reason why they do so is because they know very well that when you are successful, they will tell people that they helped you by taking decisions for you. Sometimes in life you might end up doing things in order to fit in where you don't belong to please people. You will ensure that you don't disappoint the people you are trying to please in order to be loved. You will put more effort on what they told you to do while your time is being wasted.

Sometimes you need to forget about those around you and focus on your future and desires. Your own desires are the most precious things which are not meant to be compared to what a man can give you, Respecting your own desires is like building a house on a rock which will make your house stronger forever. But compromising your own desires for the sake of a man is like building a house on sand. You must understand that your own desires are important than other people's desires. You don't need to blame your self because of what happened in the past, don't blame yourself for the decisions you took in the past.

You need to have great faith in order to achieve your goals and not someone else's goals, when you don't have faith it's probably obvious that you will do what please people, because it shows that you don't know yourself. Even God Says "it is impossible to please him without faith" it's impossible to please yourself without faith. You don't need to go to the shop to purchase faith, FAITH COMES BY HEARING.
Don't let opportunities pass you by, while doing other people's will, You need to ask yourself questions like, if I am not doing what I love who will do it for me?
If I do what pleases others who will do what pleases me?

You don't need someone to take decisions for you, remember you survived nine months in your mother's womb alone, they were not there for you, so why do you need them now?

Live a life that will please you and not a men. the frog started to realise that pleasing other animals is useless and it's a waste of time, But it had no choice, but to please other animals. The frog tried to bring hope and strength in its own life by pleasing other animals, but it could not do so. The frog said: "I won't let peace pass me by".

My life would have been better if I had peace.

I prefer having peace for the rest of my life, than be happy because happiness is unreliable but peace is reliable.

I can not guarantee happiness but I can guarantee peace, "I rather have peace than have happiness, which does not satisfy me" the frog said.

The frog told it-self that I won't take things that does not make me a happy animal with peace anymore. While the ant was busy pushing a small round ball around, the frog was empty handed walking away from it, the ant was very furious and it started calling the frog with a loud voice but the frog did not pay attention to the ant. The ant said " **There is nothing you can by yourself ,you are just useless and worthless, you are already a failure, you have failed to find water, your abilities can never take you anywhere, you need me in your life in order to achieve greatness"**

As the frog walked towards the stream and thought to itself that maybe there's a sort of developments at the stream, unfortunately there was none. The frog was hoping for the best, but at the same time was expecting worse results, because it lacked faith. When the frog was busy walking to the stream and saw the clouds moving around and seemed as though it was going to rain, but there was no rain, the clouds gave the frog new hope and Faith. The frog knew that when clouds gather together something must happen. The frog started to proclaim things that were not visible during that time.

The proclamation came as a result of a newly injected hope and faith. The clouds gave the frog hope and faith in its current predicaments. The frog then noted that if another animal or insect experienced the same fate as that of its own, then the animal or insect would have been dead, so the frog also realised that sometimes you have to fight in order to adjust and get used to an unfamiliar environment in order to reach your goals.

You need to understand that you don't have to please anyone to reach your destination, You need to please yourself and you will be satisfied. Don't expect things to come easy in your life, do not expect things to come easy, because things that comes easy are not permanent. Permanent things always take time to come, be patient and wait for them. You don't need to sit down and say I'm being patient; you need to work and suffer for a long time.

Being patient is not synonymous to sitting down and doing nothing; it means suffering and working hard daily, while expecting good things to come to your life.

Not everyone will be in bad predicaments, but if you find yourself in a bad predicament, then know that you are chosen and you are the right person to accomplish a purpose within that predicament. You can do all things even though you may pass through difficult predicaments. A dysfunctional environment is not always there to prevent you from achieving you dream.

Your predicament can only narrate your past, but has no ability to define your future. You can do it and you can achieve it despite all the limitations that limit others. You can expand your limitations to become limitless. Everyone is born with a purpose, but 85 % does not want to follow their purpose, they are limited by their environment, while 10% is willing to live their purpose, but they get discouraged by negativities around them and only 5 % are already living their purposes, regardless of their environment or predicaments.

CHAPTER 1

Few people are determined to make their purpose to be what they want to live. Your purpose and your dream are what makes you relevant here on earth, don't take someone's dream thinking it might match your purpose. Your Dream and purpose share the same patterns, they are related and they complete each other. You might complete your dream when following a crowd, but you cannot complete the pattern of your purpose when following a crowd.

The reason why people hates the activity you've started it's simply because they cannot start their own things, their jealousy has made them forget that they can do something, for as long as they are still alive. Their jealousy has blinded them and made them haters. People who hate others are the same people who have abilities to do something, unfortunately it is not easy for them to realise that they can do something. Don't allow haters to stop from achieving your dream. If you want to live a peaceful life don't hate anyone even when you are wronged. Work on your dream!

You cannot reach your dream when you are afraid of your haters and you cannot reach your dream when you feel like you are not enough. Everyone is complete, you don't need any addition for you to reach your dream. If you start to hate others, you will feel insufficient. Jealousy is a way of proving that somebody is feeling insufficient. **If you are capable of doing something, you will never feel insufficient.** Confidence gives you the ability to be sufficient and complete.

CHAPTER 2

Use Your Qualities

We all want to live a better life and we all want to achieve what seems great and what will change our lives for better. It is our responsibility to build our lives by using our qualities, for our qualities qualifies us to have dreams that we can achieve. We must live life based on the qualities we have, we don't need to imitate animals by trying to use the qualities of animals, as human beings God gave us our own qualities. Discipline is one of the qualities that you should have by being a disciplined person, if you are not disciplined you will end up being destitute.

You will lack important things if you don't discipline yourself, nobody can teach you discipline or tell you to become disciplined, you have the power to teach yourself discipline and be disciplined for the sake of your character, you cannot have a good character if you are not disciplined.

Discipline is the foundation or root of character and character is the stem of integrity. Character has the power to influence you to grow, you cannot have a good character and not grow. You cannot hide character, in order to see that one has a good character; their character will be displayed in their growth. Where there is no good character, there is no growth. Good character attract growth. Just look around you, people who reject you are the people who lacks good character or you are the one who lack good character. For one to have moral principles he or she must first be disciplined. I have met a lot of people who are not disciplined, who are seeking integrity in the absence of discipline. Integrity requires discipline. Discipline is an integral part of integrity.

Qualities of life are the source of our dreams, for your dream to become real, it has to rely on the qualities you have, for they will accelerate your dream and make it become reality through you. You have the power to dream and your qualities have the power to support your dream. If your dream is not supported by your qualities then your dream is not real or you don't use your qualities in a good manner, for you cannot build or reach a dream without discipline. Discipline sharpens you for your dream.

Let's look at a tree, what makes a tree grow are: water, soil, sun and roots. Every tree should grow from the ground, the soil is the environment of a tree and incubator of the roots of the tree, it means if there is no soil the roots cannot be strong, we may not see the roots but they play an important role on the tree. Water accelerate the roots and provokes the growth of the tree and the sun is an acid that give the tree hope that it will produce the fruits. These are the qualities a tree has to grow based on. The soil disciplines the roots of the tree, if the soil is not good for the tree, the tree will be undisciplined, for it will not grow well and it will not produce fruits.

What are your qualities? you cannot live this life without qualities, because you will suffer when you reach your breaking-point. Your breaking-point requires your qualities, such as faith. When you don't have a good character that will represent you when you reach your breaking-point, then you will never be broken.

 Character is one of your qualities, it is the most important quality that you should use most times, because it is your image. You are nothing if your image does not represent you well in the society, you should have a good image. Good reputation is the results of having a good character that will enable you to have a dream that will not benefit you alone, people with selfish dreams lack good character.

Sometimes having a bad character might lead one to have dreams that are not good for the community they live in. If you want to be respected have a good character and respect others who are also working toward reaching their dreams.

When God created a human being the aim was not just to create a human, but to impart the human being with qualities that will help the human being take care of the earth that he created. The earth was created for a human and the human was created for the earth, the earth is dysfunctional without a human being and the human being is dysfunctional without the earth. For a human to showcase he needs to be here on earth and for the earth to produce fruits there should be a human being who sow the seeds of the desired fruits.

To be a man there are qualities behind him that qualifies him to be a man. The above mentioned qualities will help you believe in your dream, only if you possess them. When you want to cross the dam it's either you swim or use a boat to go to the other side of the dam, when you have the mentioned qualities you will be able to have many strategies to do something that others cannot do. People love using popular strategies. Always remember that popularity does not always mean the best. Every strategy that is known by many is crowed, because it's easy to imitate, I cannot deny the fact that we have been taught to do simple things only because we are too lazy to put efforts, but it is high time for us to do what seems difficult, so to break the "difficulty" concept.

CHAPTER 3

Never Entertain Excuses, Be Focus!

Complaining is not good for someone who has faith, but it is good for someone who does not have faith. You need to understand that when you complain while you have faith you are cursing your own blessings, don't curse yourself by complaining. Complaining will always discourage you and you will end up giving up on your dreams. Stop complaining if you want to have a better future. You need to know that complaining will create in you the habit of giving excuses. Excuses are not good because they destroy dreams; dreams do not come easy, if you don't make them your first priority. Don't let your dreams slip away from you, keep your dreams in your mind daily, don't spend a day without thinking about them.

Refuse to be fooled by your current challenges. Before you can wake up in the morning think about your dreams, think about where you want to be in the next seven years. Make everyday be the day victory, even though things are not going well, pretend as if things are okay. Don't let your enemy (Difficulties) know your weak point, because your enemy will always attack you at your weak point. Don't be weak, but be determined.
Make sure that nothing stops you from achieving the unachievable, do things that seems to be impossible. Don't let your environment determine your future, Your environment might be undeveloped, but use the little knowledge you have to cope in your environment, don't let what is happening in your environment affect you. Wake up! see beyond your environment. Be a dreamer don't be limited by the things you have, make sure that what you have contribute towards your future.

You cannot build your tomorrow with things that you don't have, but you can build your tomorrow using what God gave you.

It might be a talent, develop that talent and make it functional and useful in your life. There are many talents that are neutral today because they lack development.

Don't do something because you want it to be a backup, if you do so you will be wasting your time, follow your dreams, make every minutes of your life useful. Make sure that you are effective and productive, produce good fruits that will build your future.

Many people want to start businesses, but they cannot start because they have been told that business demands a lot of money while it's wrong. In life we normally want to do big things, but do not know the principle which says **(start with small things if you want to do big things in life).** Lacking awareness that you cannot start big things in the beginning, you have to start small. Lacking money is an excuse for those who find it more entertaining than their dreams.

Remember doing nothing everyday doesn't only affect your body, but also affects your thinking capacity, because when you do nothing daily you are draining your brain. Avoid excuses if you want to succeed in life, I know the road seems to be long but keep on trying. People have the idea of planning but at the end of the day, they fail to plan and this thing also kills dreams.

You need to let go of things that discourage or destroy you, let it go you don't need things that are against your dreams. Produce clear pictures in your mind of where you want to be. The difference between who you are is what you do to be where you want to be and what you have to do to be where you dream to be in the future.

You must understand that your dreams can not come easily if you don't create a clear image in your mind about them. Speak everything you want to achieve in the future, speak them fearlessly. When you speak things that you don't have you confuse the enemy (Problems or Difficulties).

Sometimes you need to stay away from people who want you to help them do their own will, while you are not doing yours. The people around you only know you, but God knew you, meaning he knows your destination. Those people around you can only narrate your past, but they cannot write your future. Leave them and focus on your dreams and desires. Your desires are more important to your life and they can have an impact in your life only if you follow them.

Believe in your desires, don't let them remain as desires only, make sure that your desires contribute towards your dreams. There is a danger of having desires that are not related to your dreams, you cannot achieve your dreams if your desires are not related to your dreams, they have to correspond and work together for your good. When your desires and dreams are related you will never go wrong in life.

Remember everything you need in life are there, but it takes courage to recognise them. Your courage will take you to a place of perfection (DREAM LAND) Let your courage transform your life by taking you to your designated place or destiny. You can go far and achieve a lot. We as people have one common desires, which is to be wealthy, but not all of us will be wealthy because some of us have the desire to be wealthy while we are not acting towards being wealthy, the only thing that many people do is to talk about how wealthy we want to be, **(words without deeds are like a room without doors and windows.)** People often say that "Actions speaks louder, than words"; I agree with them. Being fruitful begins when your desires correspond to your dreams, having a desire is normal, but dreaming is extraordinary.

For a person to dream he needs the foundation of desiring extraordinary things. Desires and dreams are twins, you cannot dream if you don't desire and you cannot desire if you don't dream.

When the frog was on the way to the stream saying "indeed life was never meant to be easy it was meant to be hard at the beginning, but at the end to be easy, sometimes I should endure pains in order to have access to victory, because there is no victory without pains. My problems are like washing machines, they twist, spin and knock me down I don't know whether I will come out clean or brighter than before, but I believe that this is preparation for the future. I think this is preparation, because in order to have a future you should prepare, without preparation it is impossible. The frog was conscious when it was walking through the pain that was taking control upon it. The frog was conscious it had positive thoughts about its future.

The frog realised that ahead of every long journey there is a great life filled with Joy and peace, the frog kept on walking to the stream like a somnambulist. The frog was taking slow steps in order to save energy for another day so that it could survive the following day. The frog knew that if it could find water its own problems will end, but the frog knew that EVERY MAN HAS A DESTINY. The frog believed in two things while it was walking, the frog believed that maybe it could die or find water in a stream. On the other side the frog was overwhelmed with joy, because it was doing something that satisfied it.

As a human being you cannot be overwhelmed with joy if you are not doing what satisfies you, if you want happiness to rule in your heart, do what you are passionate about, don't be induced to do what takes you out of your satisfaction, by doing the following you will never attracts any barriers.

Most barriers in life are attracted to meaningless things, things such as **I can't, I cannot, I won't be able, I am not the right person to do this and I wasn't born to do this.**

When you say these words above, you start attracting barriers to hamper you from going further, there are many people out there who have failed because of the words above, the moment you start speaking these words you attract failures which leads to frustration. Be careful of what you say in life concerning your future, because it might demolish or dilute your dreams or your future. The frog has never thought of giving up because it was too early for it to give up. The frog knew that if it could give up it will disappoint itself that's why the frog never thought of giving up.

The frog was not going to benefit if it had to give up, because those who give up are not sure about themselves and they have low self-esteem. The frog wanted to prove that the challenges do not limit it to go further. A frog realised that a man who is limited by the challenges is not a man, because a man should conquer challenges over and over. The frog knew that a man who uses his own muscles to prove that he is strong he is not a man, because a real man is defined by actions and words. The frog wanted to be a man of actions. The frog also realised that a man is not a man without his own thoughts, because a man is controlled by his own thoughts. The frog said: "I will not let my experience limit me to go further and I will not let my habit control my thoughts".

The frog realised that a man controlled by his habit is more useless than a drunken man.
The frog knew that a positive mind always have positive thoughts which brings positive outcomes, as a result making a future possible. The frog had positive thoughts towards its future and also believed that challenges are announcement of where you are going.

The more the challenges you have the more you will become great and strong in the future. Already the frog had confidence concerning its future; confidence always brings peace and joy in life. Confidence is one of the qualities of believing in yourself when nobody does.

The frog found peace, because of self identification and for casting its sights unto the Lord. Reason why the frog had peace it is because it knew itself, the frog made self-introspection by looking upon the face of the Lord. The face of the Lord gave the frog qualities and thought it how to survive in the dessert. One other thing the frog discovered is that DON'T GRAB OPPORTUNITY BECAUSE YOU ARE DISPARATE. Desperation will also cause desperation for your future, because everything that is done in desperation will also bring desperate results.

The frog received the reflection of itself from the face of the Lord because it was able to receive. It is impossible to receive when you don't understand what receiving is; you cannot understand what is receiving is when you don't believe. It is impossible to believe when you don't have faith and you cannot have faith when you don't know the steps of having Faith. The frog knew all the steps of faith before it had faith.

The frog was busy walking and something dropped in its mind, something which is more important and it was something that was going to change its life. The frog realised that it is important to have a vision, so that you can have direction in life. It is not easy for a man to know the direction when he doesn't have a vision and it is also important for a man to have a vision, because a vision will bring light to the blind and also it will help a man to understand his journey. A man who does not understand a vision is a fool because a man is meant to understand a vision.

It is important as a man to know where you are going and be able to pave your way to your future. The only weapon to pave a way to a future is a vision.

Your vision will usher you to your future and it will help you cope with every situations you face along the way and will be able to understand that preparation for future is not about sitting down and doing nothing, but by paving your way towards your future and future is not a destiny. Future is where you are going to be tomorrow or next year, but destiny is what your life will be.

A real human being must have an accurate vision for himself or herself. A person without a vision he's like a lost ship in the middle of the sea without a destination. Vision is what speaks to you when you are quiet. Vision is what changes your perspectives about life. Have a genuine vision, vision is something that stirs you daily, a genuine vision provokes you to sacrifice when you need to, you don't sacrifice for meaningless things.

 Vision has necessities that frustrate undisciplined people. You cannot tell an undisciplined person about courage and character, that person will not understand and Listen to you. Some had glorious and marvellous vision's unfortunately they went to the grave with their vision's, because they have never made their vision's to be massively massive ,reason being they have never sacrificed for their vision. Don't be like them be different, be the owner of your vision and take charge.

Their visions was the only way for them to turn around their lives but they messed up by being ignorant, they didn't believe in sacrificing for their visions **If you don't sacrifice for your Vision you will be tormented by what life gives you for the rest of your life .** When you don't have a vision you will know all the aspects of hard times.

                                                    CHAPTER 3

What you do when your Vision is neutral will torment you for the next few years, what you ignore for the sake of your Vision will not come near you, for what you ignore contradicts your Vision and your Vision cannot accommodate that thing then you will be safe. **Expose yourself to environment that are related to your dream** E.g. when you want education ,you should go to school and study in order to get education. When you want to hear the word of God, you go to the house of the Lord and Listen to the word of God in order to grow up Spiritually but when you need petrol you go to the filling station, so should you expose yourself to environment that corresponds with your vision. When you don't expose yourself to environment which match your vision you are creating barrier to your vision .

A vision is not meant to distrust a man, but a vision is meant to help a man to be able know his way. A vision works like a guide that helps the ship. A man is ushered by a vision and a vision gives a man boldness in order to be able to stand every storm that comes along the way. Vision gives strength and boldness. A vision is like an engine which drives a man to reach his desires and helps a man to take responsibilities of his decisions. It is important for a person to know the values of having a vision about his or her future.

The frog had an exciting vision about its own future and the frog was very happy to have its own vision. It is important for you as a person to have your own vision and be responsible for your vision. Never be a person who has anything is his mind, be a man who is still and who is able to use his senses in order to pave way for his future. Let your vision encourage you; never let your current sufferings discourage you. Let your thoughts guide you all the times, then you will be able to understand that it is important to listen to your thoughts and also it is very good to pave your future by having a vision.

Don't entertain negative thoughts about your future, entertain positive thoughts about your future and remove bad habits in your mind. The mind does not only help you remember what happened in the past, but the mind helps you arrange life in order to make you prosperous. It is important for you to sometimes sit alone and spend time thinking. Do not compete with anyone, but compete with yourself, because there is a danger when competing with someone else, you might end up making wrong decision. Having a future that you have never sweat for is like living in a house that does not belong to you.

It is very important to be diligent, to look ahead and plan ahead about your future, never plan something to gain temporary happiness. Plan a good thing that will contribute toward your future. Don't expect to reap something you never sowed, prepare for your future when you still have the strength.

Preparation is the key to success and an essential tool for preparation is determination. Don't let anyone prevent you from doing what could build your life and future, don't listen to people who always discourage you from doing what is more important in your life.

Never accept what they say about you when you try to have a different vision from theirs, be a person who do not comprise on your vision for the sake of the people around you and don't feel guilty when they don't understand or love your vision. Remember not everyone will use the same ladder to reach the top, everyone want to be at the top and don't be fooled when they tell you that you have to use the same ladder they have used to get to the top. Be transformed and create your own ladder and opportunities to get to the top; don't wait for people to tell you that there is an Opportunity for you.

Always remember that excuses are the enemy of your Vision, the moment you start making unnecessary excuses is the moment you develop unwanted habits for your life, those habits will start controlling and manipulating you and compelling you to go in the wrong direction. Many people went to the grave with their dreams, reason being they allowed excuses to shift them to the direction that is too dangerous for their dreams and that is why they never accomplished their dreams.

Disadvantages Of Comfort zone

Life is shapeless, it cannot define what success is, most time people say life is unfair, yes it's true life is unfair, it cannot feel pity for you. If you think that life will be your friend then you are allowing life to influence you with the word "Impossible", this word has led many toward destitution, instead of following their dreams.

Most people are more concerned about being comfortable, they want to feel relaxed, the more you are relaxed the more life drains you and weakens your mind. If you are not ready to feel the pain then you will suffer from a disease called regret. Being comfortable is a simple thing, that is why it does not benefit anyone. Most people who are comfortable about where they are, they are not aware of the process that is damaging them, for they are comfortable, when you are comfortable, everything seems to be good to you, you can end up associating yourself with pig's.

You cannot sense the environments that are good for you when you are comfortable, being comfortable makes you ignorant most of the time. It is highly impossible to plan and dream when you are stuck in your comfort zone. You cannot be challenged in your comfort zone, nothing will challenge you because you are caged. It won't be necessary for you to dream. In the comfort zone there is no time to have goals, for they won't be necessary for you.

The comfort zone will silence you; You cannot speak the language of where you want to be when you are in the comfort zone. You cannot even be open minded, comfort zone will say no to you, for it doesn't allow you to be open-minded, the only thing that comfort zone can allow you to do is being like the rest.

Nothing good can happen to you until you make something good, It's a way of being genuine, nothing happens to genuine people, but genuine people make good things. In the comfort zone, there is no creation. You cannot develop your Gifts when you are comfortable.

When I was in high school, I was too comfortable because of what I had, not knowing that I had nothing in actual fact. My parents used to do everything for me, I was never worried about what to eat during the night or what to wear, they made sure I wore new clothes, not knowing that comfort zone was playing its part, influencing me not to believe in myself. I never knew how to be open-minded; I thought that my life is fine until I passed matric in 2016, that's when I realised I was stuck in my comfort zone. When I arrived in Gauteng, I realised that it was time to leave my comfort zone and discomfort myself in order to achieve one of my objectives, which was publishing a book.

CHAPTER 4

What Distances you from Your Dream?

There is always that thing that separate one thing from another. The atmosphere separate the sky and the land, actually the atmosphere makes it difficult for the sky to be part of the land, it might be for a good cause, but I don't know why the separation exist. In life there are some things that often distance us from our dreams and we are not aware of that and if we don't deal with them we will fail to achieve our dreams.

If you want to become the best version of yourself it does not mean you have to undermine others. In order for you to go somewhere you have to travel for a short or long period so that you can cut off the distance between you and the desired destiny. There are many things draining our values, which should be cut off, but sometimes we are not aware that these things are too poisonous.

Remember physical appearance does not define the inward. Be careful these things might be the reason why we do not advance in life, let's us examine, what have they improved in our lives since they became part of us?

The solution would be to cut them off. I believe they are the reason for our stagnation in life. They need to be cut off. Anything that does not add value in your lives downgrades the standard of life. When a fisherman wants to fish, he uses a hook in order to fish and he does not fish without expectations. He expects the hook to catch the fish for him, but he has to control the hook so that it might catch the fish. The fisherman knows what the fish eat, he uses that in order to attract the fish. Once the fish is near to the hook it might be caught.

The fisherman will start rolling the string slightly that makes the hook in order to get the fish. The process is not easy it needs a lot of concentration, the fish might get a chance to escape or the hook might get damaged.

The fisherman rolls the string slightly in a good manner so that he might catch the fish. When he rolls the string he decreases the distance between him and the fish. Same applies to you, decrease the distance you have between you and your dream. Be focused! That distance needs to be travelled by you alone not anybody else but you. If you are not travelling that distance now by doing what will make your dream a reality you are busy pushing your dream away from yourself. Try by all means to take a step towards your dream on a daily bases.

Don't feel comfortable when you are not boosting your dream, just know that you are boosting something else which is not your dream. Get married to your dream, don't cheat on your dream, remove everything which takes your attention away from your dream, it is probably obvious that they don't add any effort to your dream, let your dream keep you busy more than anything else. Make sure every day you do an activity related to your dream.

The power of positive activity provokes you to believe in your dream more than before, positive activities stirs what is inside of you. When you have a dream these activities will stir it, your dream will be in a state of progress and you will develop a strong feeling about your dream.

Be the leader, follower, supporter and coach of your own dream. Play different roles for your dream, surely you will achieve it and live it while other people are busy fooling around. Many people who allowed others to discourage them are now regretting, because they are placed in failing circumstances.

Failure is a choice, by not willing to try is a choice that makes one to fail, nobody has the right to say he or she has failed by mistake, the efforts you apply speaks on your behalf; your actions might attract failure of revoke failure.

Some people are like opposition parties, it's their duty to oppose your dream but it is also your responsibility to push your dream. If you start believing what they say about your dream, it's like giving them shares in your dream. Their aim is not to build, but to destroy, they might help you build it, but they will make sure that you use wrong materials in building your dream and they will ensure that the foundation of your dream is not genuine.

They will fake it and wait for your dream to crush. Don't you know that opposition parties always celebrate the failure of the ruling party, don't give them a chance to celebrate, never disappoint your dream and don't be depress. Your dream can be exactly what it looks like in your imagination only if you distance yourself from what distance you from your dream. Life is full of entertainments, so never allow entertainments that life offers separate you from your dream. Do whatever is good to reach your dream, don't allow the entertainments of life to be the reason of your failure, don't fail your dream!
Entertainment has been a dangerous force used to repel many people from their dreams, so do not allow entertainment revoke you from your dreams, because you are not complete without your dream.

Most people are in the graves with their noble ideas, they couldn't use their ideas to build their dreams, because they allowed entertainments to fool them and drift them away from their dreams. If you are going to be entertained by entertainments more than by your dreams, then you will be digging a grave for your dream.

Don't love entertainments more than you dream. **Your dream is worthy.**

CHAPTER 5

Self Control and Discovery are necessities

The frog realised that it is important to have self-control when you have a vision, without self-control you cannot predict the future. The frog knew that every environment has its own characteristics, which can build or destroy one's future. The frog did not succumb to the pressure of its environment.
Self-control is one of the most important character every individual should possess, so to avoid one's thinking capacity and reputation. The frog realised that without self-control one could lose their thinking capacity and as consequence failure to change one's situation.

As a person it is important to know who you are in order to be able to turn impossibilities into possibilities, for nothing is impossible for anyone who is determined to achieve a dream.

It is also important to be able to handle the environment you live in, because it might shape you or destroy you and this will have an effect on your dream. Don't use an environment as an excuse for lack of self-control. Self-control allows you to focus on your vision. Self-control can give you a different perspective on your environment. When you have a different perceptive on your environment, you could be the one to change it for the good, since you are able to see the wrongs in your environment. Many have given up because their environment is not conducive for their greatness, when an aeroplane want to fly it does not fly first, it has to be in the right environment in order for it to take off, but then it's compelled to land on the ground. Same thing applies to you, get yourself in the right environment, make sure to learn things about the environment.

A baby doesn't start by walking, there is a crawling process and this process is painful, but the baby does not give up, because of the pains during this stage. The baby endures the pain in this stage until it passes. Never allow the environment to deter you to do what you believe in. Self-control is a key to realising things in a different way. Many have given up with an excuse that: "My environment does not allow me to". Do you need permission from your environment to reach your dream? well your environment will give you reasonable answers which is "You don't have enough resources". Listen to your inside voice and not your environment.

Self-control will help you maintain whatever you do with great dedication. A person who does not have self-control will not be able to see the difference between bad and good deeds. Self-control plays an important role in your life and also to people who are around you. Self-control will help you handle things which seems complicated to others, self-control will help you be able to respond or react in a good way and also in a respectable way.

Be a person who understand the quality of self-control and be able to teach others how to have self-control. A good behaviour is as a results of self-control and also this will help you develop a good character towards your goals and dreams.

Let your character always prevail, let your character push you go further and develop a good character. People who were able to achieve their dreams, had developed self-control and also were able to maintain it. The quality of a vision is not determined by what the vision holds, but by self-control of the person who has the vision in order to find provision for the vision.

Never ignore anything that disturbs you to exercise self-control, deal with the issue and build a barricade wall to protect your self-control in order to reach the vision you have about your future.

They are many ways which people use to achieve their goals, but they use strategies that could destroy their goals in the future. For you to reach or achieve your goals when you have self-control, you need determination, faith, positive thoughts and hard work.

Never let what you don't correspond with, correspond with your self-control, what you do should be common with your self-control. Vision and self-control are best friends, but if you don't maintain them in the same way you won't be able to see that they share common characteristics, which makes people effective for achieving their dreams. Vision makes a person to have a reason to live and self-control gives an individual the ability to focus on a dream.

The frog was so determined to reach its dreams, by finding water in the stream which was in the desert, the frog didn't give up because of its own challenges. The frog realised that the quality of life is not determined by what we have won, but by what we have discovered within it. The frog itself realised that it has discovered many things in its own life, for instance by living in the desert for a long time, if it was another weak animal it wouldn't have made it because some situations do not require lazy and weak people in order to be victorious.

As a person it is important to discover good things in life that could build your life and also that can build your community, discovery is the most important task that everyone should complete, discovering good things in life always gives you the ability to focus on your dreams, it's always seems as that if you don't achieve anything in life, that automatically makes you a looser, but to the contrary what makes you a looser is when you don't want to discover anything in life. To discover something which will value your life will help you to be determined, you will also grow, because you are able to discover something that people could not discover because they are too lazy to discover.

You have to check yourself, you cannot discover anything if you don't know who you are, work hard toward your self-discovery. If you don't know who you are, somebody else will give you an identity. The enemy of your destiny is your direction, the direction you take while introspecting yourself might kick you out of your destiny or push you into your destiny.

Discovery begins in our heart if we are able to know what satisfies our heart; we will be able to discover what is more important in our life time and what will make the difference in our generation. The essential tool for discovery is being patient, you have to know that discovery is not a two minutes thing, it takes time to discover anything. When you discover something there will be a whole set for that particular thing you've discovered, also when you know how to discover you will be to maintain what you have discovered

Maintaining something that you have discovered does not mean you have to sit back and watch what you have discovered, but it then becomes your duty to improve what you have discovered and take it to the next level. When you discover that you have a dream it is important to maintain your dream, putting more effort on the dream. It is never too early to discover something.

Make sure that when you discover your dream, you also acquire the skills of maintaining your dreams, because without the skills to maintain something, that particular thing will never be prosperous and effective. As a human being it is important not to entertain the pain you are going through when you try to discover something about your life. The journey of discovery does not need people who are weak and those who lack hope, because without hope, defeat is obvious it will crush your dream.

Pain often makes people weak in the spirit and it crushes down their souls, because pain is a package of discouragement that makes people to lose hope when they try to discover something about their lives.

CHAPTER 5

The reason why most people give up is not because they have limited materials to discover or achieve their dreams, it's simply because of the pain they have to go through when they take a journey of discovery in their lives, that is why their dreams do not grow. Pain is the most dangerous weapon for growth and growth is the most important tool for a better life. As a human being it is necessary not to entertain pain, it will make you take wrong decisions which will render you desperate.

When you have strong enthusiasm towards something pain cannot be a threat to you, pain cannot limit you to work hard every day. Enthusiasm gives you strength, power to focus and motivation to pursue your dreams. When you have enthusiasm you can and you will be able to achieve whatever you desire to achieve, your enthusiasm will drive you to the path of your dreams and when you are in the path of your dreams it is obvious that you will achieve them.

Hope and enthusiasm are best friends they play an important roles that always leave good effects in our lives and they make us recognise ourselves before we can begin to do good deeds that can provoke our dreams and goals to come to pass.

Without hope we cannot achieve anything in life, because hope gives us the reason to wake up every morning to do something about our lives. Without hope life will be terrible and difficult, that is why it is necessary for us to have hope, hope enables a man to fight for what they want to have. Hope will help you be able to pay the price for your dreams, but without hope you will not see a reason to pay the price for your dreams.

Hope is the engine of our lives that is why everybody needs hope to be able to focus on a dream, Hope enables a man to focus on what he want to have and achieve.

One should have hope in order to accelerate dreams. Be that kind of person who is driven by hope, you will see good results of having hope later. When you have hope you begin to develop a sound mind which is wisdom, we need wisdom because wisdom possess knowledge and direction, that means without hope you cannot have wisdom to know the direction which you should take for your future. Hope pushes away all the negative thoughts in your life and hope attracts things that are related to you dreams, that is why it is necessary to have hope.

Hopeless people will always have hopeless dreams. An hopeless person is someone who doesn't know how to plan for their future and he is unable to plan how to achieve his dreams and it is very painful not to know how to plan your future and how to achieve your dreams. You must know that when you sit down and plan your future and do not act it is as good as doing nothing, you need to take the first step about what you have planned in order to have progress.
It is also important to have interests toward your dreams, make your dreams your first priority, by separating yourself form things that are causing you to have confusion. Some people are confused because they don't know what they want in life because they are indulged in many things which brings confusion in their lives. Some people even go as further as believing other people's opinions than their own opinions. Actually they are neutral, because confusion does not bring progress, it brings stagnation.

Know your gift and add value on it, because your gift will open great doors for you. Do not depend on temporary things learn to be separated from temporary things, for temporary things always causes regrets. You need enthusiasm in order to be an achiever. Don't feel pity for yourself, treat yourself as an achiever because if you feel pity for yourself you will not do anything good because you will always have excuses that will hinder you to go further.

Don't be impeded by excuses but be challenged to go further.

Treat yourself like a slave you will see the good results of being a slave. You must work like a slave when you still have time and you will live like a king later. Build your own empire before someone builds an empire for you, do not be weak and powerless. Learn to work hard daily by taking new steps towards your dreams and goals, your actions should speak louder, than your words. Be bold enough to work like a slave, be the legend of your generation by achieving your dreams.

Be bold enough to stand up and reach you dreams, don't make excuses if you want to succeed, excuses will destroy you and crush down your positive thoughts about your dreams. Excuses are barriers that are normally experienced by many people who do not want to grow and continue growing daily.

Stand still and avoid excuses whenever you are about to take a step towards your dreams. Do not say I cannot do it, because I lack some material, rather you don't lack any material to do what you want to do, all the materials you need is within you because you are carrying something inside of you.

You need to know that you are pregnant and you are about to give birth. The thing that you desire to have you are carrying it within you like a woman who is carrying a baby within her. Know that when you start experiencing some difficulties while walking towards your dreams, you are about to arrive at your own paradise, because when a woman is about to give birth there must be labour pains.
You cannot activate your dreams when you are afraid to take some risks that seems to be dangerous. Take some risks you will see something great will happen. When a woman is about to give birth she makes sure that she endures the labour pains.

You must be able to distinguish between a good dream and a best dream, a good dream is a dream that you can achieve easily that does not require patience, but a best dream is a dream that requires dedication, hard work, patience, good habits, sacrifice and discipline. It is your choice to chose between a good dream and a best dream, but it is better to choose the best dream for it will last forever than a good dream. A person who has a best dream will be able to maintain it when things are not going well.

Don't be confused when people around you decide to take a good dream make your own decision and take the best dream so that you cannot suffer in future. Don't make a decision that you are not sure of, don't take some decisions because of peer pressure, because you will be the one to suffer the consequences of your choices. Don't allow a good dream hinder you form achieving your best dream. Move towards your best dream. Few people have best dreams, while many people have good dreams, what is good does not mean that it can satisfy you. A good dream does not have a mission, what is the mission of your dream?

If your dream does not have a mission just know that it is a good dream. It is your responsibility to give your dream a mission.

Your dream should provide to those who are down but not out, your dream has to be a motivation to those who are still in high schools. Majority of dreams do not drive young minds to desire to succeed in life, they drive young minds to have a common thing that is **(Fame)**. Show how marvellous is your dream by making it to be a best dream. Separate yourself from people who have lower dreams, they can infect you with their low dreams. Develop the sense of achieving a best dream.

The best dream will always bring best rewards that could build and strengthen you in every area of your life.

Remember that when you achieve your best dream, it will always affect your coming generations.

Have good habits for the sake of your best dream and to be able to sustain your best dream daily. For a best dream to shine you need to take care of it and maintain it daily.

Develop good habit's towards your future, don't blame other people for your habits; **Remember Habits can destroy you or develop you!**
What are your habits?

Do you have the habit of postponing, just know that you are literally creating a procrastinating habit, you are busy delaying and denying your dreams to become a reality. Do you have the habit of believing in your dream?
Then know that you are developing a strong sense of progress. Your progress must take place in your dream.

Remember to maintain your dream when you achieve them, for every dream that could be maintained remain effective and it also makes the person who has achieved it to be more prosperous. The difference between a maintained dream and the one that is not maintained is the effectiveness and the outcomes, for every dream that get maintenance produces good outcomes that benefits the person who maintains the dream.

A dream that is maintained can be seen by its outcomes. A dream that does not get maintained it's highly impossible for it to produce good outcomes. In order for you to be able to maintain your dream it's necessary to choose the dream that you desire to have, because if you choose a wrong dream that does not correspond with your ability it will finish your strength.

Every dream that a man has should correspond with his ability. It is necessary for you to be able to prioritize, don't make priority disorder for you will crush your dream and ability.
When you choose a dream you must think about your ability because you cannot not achieve anything without your ability .e.g. Don't make a decision of becoming a leader when you know very well that you don't have a desire of raising more leaders.

Be your own instructor and hold yourself accountable if only you have a desire of achieving your dreams. You will never achieve your dreams if you keep on entertaining negative words that people speak about the dream you have. What others termed impossible does not concern you, you are unique. When others end in their failure don't get discouraged.

You are not the reason why others achieved what is called failure; they did not have a good strategy to reach their dreams and do not feel pity for them when they give up from reaching your dreams first and then later is when you can feel pity for them and give them the best strategy to achieve their dreams. Never compromise your dreams by feeling pity for people who do not want to do anything about their lives.

They are not the failures but they are ignorant, because they lack the Wisdom and understanding of becoming something in life, everyone should play their part here on earth but it seems as if some people do not want to, that is why we will always have people who are barriers to our dreams because they discourage us when they get a chance to.
Never allow people to hinder you from fulfilling what you think is best for you and just value your dreams and work on yours dreams.

The reason why they discourage us is because they have got nothing to do about their lives, they believe that discouraging others will add value in their lives or they believe that discouraging others will help them make progress to their success but they don't know that they are crushing and consuming their dreams. They destroy their ability to do something that could turn their lives around.

Ignore these kind of people when if you want to achieve your dreams. They are involved in an organization which is called the destructor of dreams.

 The destructor of dreams is not meant to encourage you to reach your dreams but to destroy and crush what is in the mind of dreamer which is a dream, don't bring them closer to you but take every arrow they throw you with to make it beneficial to your progress. Don't get discouraged when they throw you with big arrows but use that arrow as a raw material of building your success, remember an arrow brings pain and pain is part of the process, so don't complain about experiencing many pains in your journey . You cannot plant a tree when you are afraid of weather conditions

You have to be willing to stand for any destruction and destruction can be defined as something that destroys anything that seems to be new but if you are willing to face a storm which is called destruction you will achieve your dreams. Every plant that sprout again faces the storm which is called destruction, because of seasonal challenges. Even you as a human being must know that seasonal challenges are going to come. Seasonal challenges does not change the way you think about your dreams, but you do change the way you think about your dreams because you think that seasonal challenges are threat to your dreams. You have to rethink your thinking in order to defeat seasonal challenges.

                                                    CHAPTER 5

Giving attention to seasonal challenges does not help you to grow but it helps you give up on your dreams. Lazy people always blame seasonal challenges for their failure like I said before failure is caused by low self-esteem. No one should blame seasonal challenges for their failure, when you fail it does not mean you are a looser. There is a process which is called rise up and sprout again, this is a time consuming process because one should identity their mistakes first. This process will renew your thoughts, strength and ability. Sprout and rise up again when you fail for the first time.

Don't associate yourself with people who will reason your dreams, they are poisonous to your dreams ~ Lethabokenedy.

It is necessary for you when you rise up and sprout to know the difference between fear and danger, fear is a choice, but danger is a reality. Danger happens when one loses hope on a dreams, when you give up on your dreams that's when you find yourself in danger of destroying what is hidden inside of you and consuming what is not part of your life. When one has a desire to give up on a dream, they start experiencing danger. Giving up on a dream will cost you much, you will start doing things which are not part of your life. Your dreams will not cost you too much because your dreams can attract provision from nowhere.

Danger is a reality, once a challenge comes towards you it's necessary to conquer the challenge because you may find yourself in Danger. Danger will weaken you and will take away your thinking ability.

Danger affect your mind-set, be careful to not give up on your dreams as consequences you will face danger for the rest of your life and danger will give birth to failure. Remember a failure can destroy other people's dreams that is why I say he is in a prison which is called danger.

Be careful when you want to give up on your dreams, think about the prison (danger), it will harm you and people around you and you will not be able to sense you are imprisoned.

The only way to avoid danger is to achieve your goals and dreams in order to be safe. Fear is a choice that is often taken by many people who do not believe in their potentials and abilities. One should be aware that fear is not real but it's a choice. Do not be frightened of doing something you desire, remember you will regret later if you choose to be afraid of achieving your dreams. Fear makes you encounter destruction when you choose it. One must be bold enough to ignore fear in order to achieve a dream.

Sometimes we want what we start to be big at the same time that is why we find ourselves overshadowed by a cloud of fear which is caused by rushing, there is no need to rush, we start small and we will do big things later, as long as we are able to handle small things, we will then be able to handle big things. You cannot take two steps at the same time, it's impossible, most of us the reason why we have fear is because we want to take two steps at the same time and it's highly impossible to avoid fear when you take two steps at the same time, fear is caused by a certain thing that will never happen. When one has fear is not because they are not bold, even bold people often do experience fear.

Being bold means being brave and confident, but when you start to do many things that are not related you will have fear, even when you are bold. Concentrate on your dreams and stop listening to negative words; you cannot focus on your dreams when there are certain negative words you often hear and when you start paying attention to your dreams.
When you follow negative words is when you give up on your dreams because you believe that your ability and potential does not matter to your dreams.

The main purpose for your ability and potential is to help you achieve, whatever you want to achieve in your life, be careful also not to use your ability and potential to destroy your dreams, but use them wisely by building up extraordinary things.

Your ability is not meant to downgrade your dream but to upgrade your dream. Your ability is meant to increase your standard. It is necessary for you to believe in your ability in order to go further than those who despise their ability. Many people uses their abilities to brag which is wrong, use your ability for a particular purpose, what is the purpose of bragging? bragging makes one to be a fool before the eyes of the wise. The reason why you have that ability is because you are capable of doing that thing that is in your mind. When you don't despise your ability you will be able to distinguish between what is real and what is possible. What is real is what most people often achieve without going through some pains, because it's real. When something is real many people love to achieve it because they have an evidence for it. They can witness that it is real, because they have achieved it. What is real is what crush our dreams because we focus on it and forget about our dreams. It is important for you as a dreamer to understand that what is real can never transport you to your destiny or your own paradise.

To be transported to large places you must believe in possibility not in what is real. What is possible is what others has termed impossible. People believe in reality and don't believe in possibilities. When you want to achieve your dreams you must stop focusing on what is real because your dreams contradict with what is real, you must believe in possibilities. Your dreams are far from what is real, but they correspond with what is possible, it is impossible to swim when you are not in the sea and also it is impossible to go into the jungle when you are afraid of living in the bush.

When you want to achieve your own unique dream you must learn to use your own strategy. Be patient when you believe in what is possible because in order for what is possible to happen there must be an element of endurance, then perseverance. Perseverance brings new strength which is needed to accelerate your ability and faith daily, for you to have new strength everyday you must learn to show great perseverance towards your difficulties that comes on daily basis.

No one can never climb a big hill when he is not willing to climb a tree with few branches ~Lethabokenedy

Achieving what is common with others does not mean you have arrived at your destiny it means you have taken a wrong path which is not meant for you, just look around you and look what you have achieved with others, Do you benefit from it ?

The mistake that we often make is to do what others do, because we don't understand our own path. Your own path is the path that leads to your own purpose; passion is the path that leads to purpose without passion you cannot arrive. You must be willing to encourage yourself when they despise your dreams, you have to be patient.

For an instance; walking under the sun is an experience that everyone has because it's real but walking in the lions territory is an experience that people don't have.
You may find that in order to achieve your dreams you must first walk in the lions' territory. For you to achieve your dreams you must suffer first and enjoy later, because it is the reality of life that one must suffer in his life, it's either you suffer when you are preparing for your dreams or you suffer after taking a wrong path that does not lead to your dreams.

CHAPTER 5

Behind every success there is a painful struggle. Many people have greater dreams but they stop trying to reach them, simply because their struggle is too deep. The deeper the struggle, the greater the dream. Struggle is a foundation of every success, success that is not based on a struggle is not genuine. Every success that is graced has its own kind of struggle. For an example: disappointment is a struggle, people who disappoint you are contributing to the foundation of your dream.

Many people do not believe in struggles, they only believe in prosperity without struggle it's not possible to prosper without struggling. Don't expect your struggle to be the same as your brother's struggles, you need to understand your struggle. Be able to identify things that you encounter in your struggle, you may find that they are shaping you for your tomorrow. Don't allow those tears to be the reason you give up, use those tears as an acid that fasten the reaction, use them to go forward.

Find the source of your struggle and deal with it first, have resolute attitude that will help you to wrestle against your struggle. Having a resolute attitude is what makes you to know how to plan before wrestling against your struggle, don't take actions without planning. Planning is the first step of defeating what seems to be a Goliath. When you want to become a struggle conqueror you must be willing to experience the struggle. You have to know all the things you may go through when you are in a painful struggle, when you know what is a struggle and also what are the attributes of that struggle you can be a struggle conqueror and you will be able to fight for your dreams and goals.

Struggle is not meant for the weak ~Lethabokenedy

When you are a weak person you will not stand during your struggle.

                                          CHAPTER 5

When things seems to be tough that's when things begin to come together for strong people who are determined to reach their dreams. Never lack confidence when things seems tough for you, be strong and face everything that seems to be tough not to be tougher later. Prepare for a season that is coming by being bold for the season that you are already in.

For every season that seems to be difficult, just know that there is a beautiful season that is coming which will change your life only if you can prepare yourself for it. The dream can never be a reality if you do not make it a reality; it will always be a dream, the moment you stand up and put more effort in your dreams that's when you begin the process of making your dream a reality.

Only the effort you put daily can make the dream you see as an extraordinary dream to be reality into your life, never accommodate negativity in your dreams, negativity will crush your dreams and destroy your ability and downgrade your potential and also make your dream to be a dream forever, learn to trust your dream before someone despise it for you, make your dreams to be the reason for you to live. Be diagnosed with positivity so that your dream can be genuine, when you are diagnosed with positivity, negativity will not harm you; positivity is a disease that impregnates one with enthusiasm and persistence. Most dysfunctional people are diagnosed with negativity. They need a medicine (Hope) that can remove negativity in order for them to be possessed with positivity.

Be goal orientated, respect what you want to achieve, order your steps towards success, honour your ability and believe in your potential. Be the first one to achieve what is unique, for that thing will also provoke other people's dreams. Some people are looking up to you; When you achieve that thing they will come to you for advises and strategies.

The reason why some people do not reach their dreams is because they despise their dreams, they don't really believe in their dreams. Everything that one does not believe in does not make sense to them. But what you believe in will make sense to you and will also be important to you.

In order for something to come to pass there must be a soul that will believe in it. A soul brings love to something that was despised. Therefore it is important for a soul to believe in its own thing and forget about what others are saying, every soul want to be the best, No soul want to be overtaken by other souls.

There will always be conflict between souls. Always try to avoid conflicts when you work on your dreams, a conflict brings discouragement, avoiding conflicts will benefits you and enable you to focus. Some conflicts will take away your strength and you will end up believing in things which are not true, reality will be your best friend because when you don't have strength to work on your dream, you will obviously downgrade your dream to match your reality and when reality overtake you, I tell you nothing that you imagine will never come to pass.

There is nothing confusing like being overtaken by reality, reality will force you to dream what is real not what is possible. Reality has overtaken many people and they ended up giving up on their dreams, that is why we have people who will discourage us because reality has overtaken them when they were trying to achieve their dreams.

Be careful not to entertain reality, for it will ruin your dreams. Don't lose focus; know that your dreams and reality do not correspond. They are contrary to each other and things that contradict each other cannot share the same room, it's either you make a room for your dreams or for realities; it's your choice to choose what's best for you. No one can force you to do something you don't want to do, unless you love it.

Destination is your choice if you don't want to choose to arrive at your destination, nobody will encourage you to arrive. Do not sit back and forget about your destiny, think deeply about your destiny each single day.

Destination will always wait for those who are willing to arrive not for those who are not ready, not those who always have doubts. Those who doubt have to know that they doubt their ability, you don't need to be famous to reach your destiny, you can reach your destiny the way you are. Don't desire to be famous when you have not yet reached your destiny, if you become famous before reaching your destiny you will think and believe that fame is your destiny and you will relax.

Fame is not a destiny it's a stage or phase. Most people have allowed fame to get ahead of them, they have allowed fame to be their dream instead of making their dream a reality. People should know and understand that fame is a result of doing great things, but dreams are not results of fame. We are living in a generation whereby everyone wants to be famous, being famous is not a problem, by being famous without achieving your dream is a problem because fame has an expiry date but your genuine dream does not have an expiry date.

97% of people who want to be famous are not willing to labour for their dreams, what is the purpose of being famous, will your fame have a great impact in people's lives? if your fame is not going to have a great impact in people's lives why should you then become famous? We don't need dysfunctional famous people who are not contributing anything in our societies. I rather contribute with my dream toward building this generation rather than seeking fame. If you are seeking to have fans instead of having a dream, then negativity has corrupted your mind. What is it that your fans are going to learn from you?

Fame is temporary but dreams are not temporary, what is temporary is for the present moment, but what is not temporary is a lifetime thing that could even create an empire or a legacy for future generations.

Concentrate on your dreams, before you concentrate on a certain stage which you can encounter in life, some stages seems as if they are our destiny whilst in reality they are not.

Make sure that when you encounter some stages in your life you don't forget about your dreams, because your dreams are more valuable than the stages that you encounter in life. There is nothing that is more precious than your dreams.

Fame can be the reason of your downfall, don't seek fame when you are not yet disciplined ~ Lethabokenedy

CHAPTER 6

Run Your Race And Reach Your Destiny

What is the purpose of running a race without patience. The outcome of a race with patience is better off, than a race without patience. Patience is the main key to unlock the capabilities of a person, patience is what transform and release somebody to do something. You cannot start building when you are not understanding the purpose of the foundation. Even in life you cannot start something without knowing that patience is the tool to build. I believe that patience is the essential layer for your foundation. When you begin to run, you must first fasten your shoes, patience symbolically speaking is your shoes, your shoes helps you to continue running even when the ground is unstable.

Confidence is the ignition key to start a race aiming to win it. When the sun rises in the morning people often gain strength because it's going to be a sunny day, when a runner has confidence to run a new race he gains new strength.
Confidence gives you ability to make you stay in the game for a long time. Don't be intimidated by other's enthusiasm when you are running your race, there are some people who are enthusiastic, but do not have confidence, that is why they end up not believing in themselves.

Know that everything you do and you are not sure about it will give you doubt, because you lack confidence that will keep you and revive you every minute you spend. It is highly impossible to regret when you have confidence, for confidence gives you the ability to stay in the game (Race). Confidence is a necessity when running a race, as people we have different races to run, but they can only happen if we are willing to sacrifice for them.

Everybody want to be the ultimate winner of the race, but not everyone is willing to sacrifice for their race. Actually not everyone is willing to match their words with their actions, because their experience limits them. You have to forget about your past experiences, because you have never experienced your destiny. Never allow your past experiences to limit you from going further.

When a runner runs a new race he forgets about all the previous races, he focuses on the new race. The previous races are not important than the race you are facing right now. Remember failure is a chance to improve but giving up is a chance to crush your race. Never allow your race to beat you, but the contrary should be the case. The only way to beat your race is knowing how to step when the race begins.

Never undermine your race, when people say you don't have an experience of doing what you are doing, you must always remember that experience can limit you to go further. The moment you start listening to people's lectures on how to run your race; that's when you put your dreams in a sinking ship. It is not your problem when people don't believe or understand your dream, it's not their race, so they cannot understand it, never bother yourself by trying to convince them to understand it or believe in your dream.

The reward that you will get is better than the price that they will get, don't let yourself be intimidated by prizes other people receives, but let other people's prizes encourage you to achieve your dream. Remember a reward is better than a prize, so don't seek prizes, but seek rewards by working toward your dream. Many people have dreams, but they don't know what are the benefits of their dreams, they can't even create clear image of their dreams, this is all caused by disorder of priorities.

Reason being is that they are competing with others. The reason why today we have many people who do not want to pursue their dreams is because, they are looking for competition instead of completion. People are wasting their time on things that do not bring good results at the end, they are committed to competition. What I have realised about people who compete with their others is that they always get hurt at the end.

Their dreams become paralyzed because you cannot compete with a genuine thing and not get hurt. Most people who compete with others are not aware that they are gambling with their dreams. They use the effort that was meant to develop their dreams toward competing with other people who do not even care about their future. **If you want to paralyze your dream, imitate those who compete with others, but if you want to see your dream being effective and productive, then embrace the idea of completing others.**

Most people play with their dreams in the name of they (cannot beat me). Remember you were in your mother's tummy for nine months alone, you were not competing with anyone, but why would you want to compete with others here on earth?
In your mother's womb you were able to spend nine months in your mother's womb, you were not in a hurry to be born, because you knew that you were going to be placed in an incubator, even now don't compete.

Competition To Fulfil Your Dreams

Many people are looking for competition, because they have been taught that competition is good, which is not good for somebody who's aiming to achieve something in the end. competition is something very interesting, but it's also something that can delay you or dilute you, because the aim of competition is to give an individual a noble prize and this is where most people are limited.

Being in competition to achieve your dreams is a waste of time and energy. Competition is for people who are not sure about their dreams. Why are you following the crowd, why don't you stand on your own and leave others indulge in unnecessary competitions.

Most people do not reach their dreams, because they have the habit of competing. Break that habit of competing with others, develop the habit of completing other. There are those who compete by drinking alcohol. The money that they spend on alcohol could be used to invest in their dreams.

Competition Of Dreams

One has to desire to complete what he or she started in order to go far. People are lazy to complete, but they are not lazy to compete. you need to have a character of completing other; it is very challenging to finish what you have already started because life punches us with difficulties and discouragements. But it takes a disciplined and focused person to endure those things and conquer them.

Those difficulties are only there to tell you that you are about to arrive where you are going. It is your responsibility to complete your dream. Be the owner of your dream, achieve it, reach it and live it. When you are not completing others, you are giving failure to associate with you. Use whatever you have to complete that your dream, people might think that your dream is something that will never come to pass or exist but I am here to tell you that you are about to experience that dream, just do not give up on it.

You might not be able to touch your dream but it doesn't mean you cannot reach it, you can reach it but only if your effort is consistent. Paint your dream in your mind, see it massively in your mind, for anything you can perceive, you can have. **when you want to achieve a Dream, you place yourself into the realm of dreams and choose your dream. The aim is not to compete, the aim is to complete and the purpose is to reach it.**

CHAPTER 7

Break The Camp And Move On!

You have been there for a long time and you have been there like a tree which cannot move. You do not have limitations, you can do anything, you are not like a tree. Most people do not want to leave their comfort zones, because they are afraid to start new comfort zones. Go and make your own comfort zone, you don't belong where you are, it's not the right place for you, Just look around, what have you done since you lived in that comfort zone?
You have probably done nothing because you do not belong there. The moment you leave that place you will realize who you really are.

The moment you break your camp and go forward with your life without them you shall see that you can do what you thought you couldn't do before, actually right now you are in a nest, you want people to tell you what to do. Leave that nest start being independent, you will never achieve your dreams if you hate being independent, independency brings freedom to your dreams. When you still depend on people, they will not allow you to dream they will dream on your behalf and they will tell you what is good for you and not what is best for you. You have to leave people who do not wish you the best, for they are not your destiny helpers, if they were your destiny helpers they were going to help you achieve best things in life.

If they induce you from believing that there is no real meaning of quality of life, they are your enemies, if they don't want you to live a life of fortune, they are fake, leave them and be independent. Never be deceived, if you do more for them and they do less for you, just know that they are dysfunctional, leave them.

stand on your own and do things that will attract growth in your life. Don't stay in your comfort zone thinking that people around you will be phenomenal, leave them be phenomenal you will attract phenomenal things. Being phenomenal is not about having tangible things, but it's about believing in what you do even when nobody does.

It's about doing what you love when there is no one who is watching, when you break the camp no one will notice you, they will think that you are confused, leave the camp alone. Don't mind what they are saying, they will say hopelessness is the reason why you've left them. Actually they are confused, because they don't believe in greatness, they believe that staying in the same place will help them to go further, which is not good. Don't break the camp with anyone, break it alone.

People love gatherings, remember in a gathering others get transformed and others get lost, if you really want to achieve your dreams, learn to isolate yourself from people who are lost or who are dysfunctional, remember dysfunctional people can affect you to be like them. The more you associate yourself with them, they impart what is in their minds and you will be at the same level with them, because a group of confused people is more dangerous, than a single confused individual.

E.g. Nowadays young people often say we can achieve other things without education, it's true! But the purpose of education is to give everyone knowledge, for the purpose of knowledge is to help one to be able to sustain or maintain one's life. You can achieve something without education, but you will lack the ability to maintain it. Don't be like those who despise education, respect education and love education. Those people you are associated with are not looking to go further, they are not going anywhere. Do they speak about their goals or they are just waiting for manna from heaven, remember God helps those who help themselves and those who work hard.

People who are going somewhere are people who are not comfortable about where they are. Among men who know the thoughts of man except the spirit within him, know one knows. You may find that they don't want to go anywhere, because they have already given up on life, but don't allow them to infect you with their disease of giving up on life. Know that you are worthy when you are working towards achieving your dreams. Always remember that a disease of giving up in life is called laziness. Never allow the disease of laziness to affect you, believe that you are not lazy but a hard worker.

People who are lazy for their dreams are lazy for their destines, they need to wake up ,but what I love about them is that the moment they realise that you are going far ,they are going to join you, because they will feel like they are left behind. The more they join you they provoke you to continue working towards your dreams. Be responsible for your growth each single day, the more you grow, the close you are to your dream. Growth is the assurance, which confirms that you are ready to live your dream.

They will despise your dream, but don't entertain them. Remember in the bible there is a story about a boy who was called Joseph; A young man who had a dream when he was sleeping, a best dream and when he woke up he shared his dream with his brothers. They started despising his dream and said "Who are you to dream stars and the moon because among us we have dreamt the same dream not what you are talking about". When you dream something that is more marvellous people around you will start questioning you. This happens when you leave your comfort zone. When Joseph's brothers were despising his dream, he was in the process of leaving his comfort zone.
When they despise your dream they are actually giving you an opportunity to break the camp. Break that camp if you want to go far.

CHAPTER 8

Be A Leader Of Your Dream

The real quality of a leader is not determined by the number of followers he has but by how he leads his followers (Dream). I believe that we are called to be leaders, we can all lead our dreams, when we lead our dreams we will see the skills of leadership within us, only our dreams can prove or show the level our leadership. Don't wait for someone to appoint you as a leader No!

If you want to become a leader lead your dream.

The moment you wait for people to appoint you as a leader, it's like waiting for the sun in the middle of the night knowing very well that the perfect time for the sun is the day not the night. Lead your dream then your dream you will give you an opportunity to be recognised by people who need a leader who can lead them to reach their dreams, then they will appoint you as their leader. I was not aware that leading my dream could open an opportunity for me to become a leader, until I was appointed as a youth leader where in my local church, then I discovered that the best way to become a leader is by leading your dream first.

During that time my dream was to become a motivational speaker for the youth then I started having this passion, I used to send motivational speeches on Whatsapp on daily basis, that's when they saw potential in me of becoming a leader, then I was appointed as a leader. Lead your dream first you will see the power of leading your dream. Age does not matter but what matters is the level of your maturity. Be committed to your dream and value your dream with good character that will uplift what you believe in.

Being enthusiastic begins when you believe in your dream, don't say I am enthusiastic when you don't show your enthusiasm anywhere. Be an enthusiastic person who can use his enthusiasm where it's necessary.

Leadership is not about experience, nor by age but by doing what will make the **will** to come to pass. A leader doesn't need to have muscles but to be intellectual in every aspect of the dream. A blind leader always tries to bring what is not necessary in a dream, You cannot bring a football player in a netball game, this two things opposes each other. Learn to accommodate things that will contribute to your dream. Some leaders have associated themselves with things that brings confusion into their dreams, that is why they are not productive in every aspect of their dreams, they are stagnant, because they have accommodated stagnation in their dreams.

A leader doesn't need to be neutral or stagnant, but a Leader has to be active and bring changes, changes that will develop a dream to grow. A leader cannot do this all when he doesn't know the purpose of being a leader. A great leader knows the mandate of leadership. Don't lead without a mandate. Some leaders are being threatened to be removed from their positions of leadership, because they lead without a mandate.

Accomplishing, reaching and achieving your dream is your own mandate for now, never allow those who lead without mandate to frustrate you or pull you back from performing your task. We are living in an era whereby Leaders want things to be done in order to get recognitions. **Don't allow fame to get ahead of you.** A leader that seeks fame is a baby leader, he is not fit to be in a position of leadership. His behaviours are still childish.

Lead your dream with maturity, lead your dream as an organization and never undermine your leadership skill.

CHAPTER 8

Remember you were able to lead yourself for the first time, when you were coming out of your mothers womb during birth, why can't you lead the dream you now have and make it to be effective so that it can bring positive impacts in other people's lives. A leader of a **Dream** doesn't allow difficulties to refrain him from reaching a dream. When you lead, know that you will encounter difficulties, those difficulties are only there to test your leadership skills, but if your leadership skill is weak you will not conquer those difficulties.

A real quality of leadership is determined by having a strong **Bond** of leadership. Those who claim to be investors for dream, don't them bring closer to you they are not your dream helpers, a dream helper doesn't seek attention. Those who need attention are not the right people to invest in your dream. Some companies are falling apart because leaders have accepted unwanted or unnecessary Investors who seeks attention and not affection.

Don't allow everyone to be involved in your **Campaign (Dream)** if you want to do your own thing alone, is not a bad idea to lead alone, actually is a good idea, no one will undermine your decisions at the end of the day. Don't allow rumours to mislead you, lead according to the mandate and the rumours will do you no harm or the rumours will be harmless to you. Those who are misled by rumours cannot lead and go far. Focus on your mandate and ignore all those negativities. A leader who entertain rumours more than his mandate will end up succumbing to the rumours, remember what you don't overtake, will in turn overtakes you.

Don't be a leader who does not believes in his follower (dream), but be a leader who believes in his follower (dream), believe that you are in that position of leadership because you want to achieve your best dream. If you can dream it, surely you can reach it and have it. Claim what is rightfully yours, that dream is yours and God gave you that dream, because he first believed in you.

Believe that you can achieve it by using your own skills of leading. Never mind what people say about you and your dream.

If you do not lead your dream there are vultures that will come to lead your dream and make it a sinking ship. When they become leaders of your dream, they don't do what will establish the dream, but will do what will establish them and forget the main focus. Many people have allowed people to lead their dreams and now their dreams are dead. Don't allow people to tell you how your dream should look like, you may have the idea of starting a business, but don't allow people to come and change your idea of business. We are living in the environment whereby everyone wants to benefit from others.

Let your dream be invariable when the storm comes. Don't allow the Storm (false accusations) to shake your dream, it might cause a permanent damage. I believe that before the Strom occurs there are signs that shows the Strom is ahead, if you can see those signs be prepared for the Strom ahead in order to defeat the Strom, because preparation is better than suffering. When you are prepared for the Strong, I can guarantee that you are going to conquer it.

Sometimes leading a dream might be challenging thing to you, remember every challenging thing produces good results that will affect you with clarity.

Don't be tempted, don't allow a stranger to lead your dream. Many say divine partnership is good for reaching dreams, it might be good at the beginning but it doesn't end well. People will mostly turn to be jealous. Divine partnership is not suitable for every dream. Express your individuality through your dream and you will see that you can do it. I don't know what kind of dream you have, but I can guarantee you that it's possible and reachable. Don't try to make people understand your dream, leave them and build your dream.

it takes a bird to build its nest on a tree that has got thorns, why can't you build your dream even though they say you cannot do it in a given environment, don't do things based on what your environment says, you will never do everything well in your life. Many stopped before they started because they allowed negative people preach to them. **Beware of those who preach negativity to you.**

CHAPTER 9

Attack The Storm

Don't be more conscious about the Storm than you are about your dream, in the Storm there is no time to feel pity for yourself, it's time to show what you are made off and don't be terrified by the Strom that won't last even for two hours, usually the Strom last for few minutes. When you are in the Strom don't call for help, you have to remember what got you into the storm.
In order to defeat the storm, you must fight therein, only the storm can prove the level of faith you have in yourself, if you don't believe that you can defeat the Strom, the storm will defeat you. The Storm might be there to develop your faith in your dream.

We all need the Strom that will sharpen our faith, when there is nothing that sharpens us, it's not going to be easy for us to believe in our dreams. Storms are the only avenues to develop us and also give us courage to focus on our dreams, remember the Storm is there to teach you a lesson that will be useful in your dream. Everything that happens in the Storm are easy to remember, but the things that happens in the rain are not easy to remember, because when you are in the rain you carry an umbrella, unfortunately in the Storm you cannot wear an umbrella, the wind will take away the umbrella.

The lessons that are in the storm are different with lessons that are in the rain. In the Strom you cannot observe and feel what is happening but it does not mean you have to give up, in the Strom there is betrayal. Don't let the betrayal that is in the Strom compel you to reject the calling (dream). If you can survive the Storm, I guarantee you success. Nobody survives the Storm and not succeed in all they do.

You might be struggling to set your priorities and that might be your type of Storm, but don't give up, set them again until they are in correct order.

You might be struggling to get a job, but don't give up, keep applying for until you get employed. if you don't apply for that Job know that your dream of working is going to fail. it does not matter how many people have already applied for that Job, remember persistent people do not do things simply because others are doing it. Be persistent, do it in the Storm, if you fail to do it in the Strom, you cannot do it in the rain, because in the rain there is a comfort zone which is the umbrella. You cannot do anything in your comfort zone.

We all feel comfortable in the rain, because we have umbrellas to hide ourselves, but nobody feels comfortable in the Strom, because the Strom challenges us to prove who we are. The only place that you are able to know what you are made off is in the Storm. The Strom doesn't care whether you are a billionaire or you are broke, the storm attacks you, but if you fail to attack the Strom you will never know the power you have with.

Don't run away when you are in the storm. I remember when I started to write this book, I used to discourage myself and I was not aware that actually I was in a Strom. I thought this book cannot reach many lives, because I am not well known and I am just an ordinary guy who grew up in the village until I realised that potential doesn't depend on any environment, I became more interested in writing this motivational book.

Your potential doesn't depend on where you were born or where you live, but you can expose yourself to places that will challenge and provoke your potential. You are more than capable of defeating the storm.

When you are in the storm, it's an opportunity for you to express your power.

Don't be moved by the Strom, but be encouraged by the Storm to fulfil your dream. I don't know what kind of dream you have, but you cannot achieve it only if you run away from the Storm, the Storm is not there to punish you, but it's there to prepare you. The Storm does not dilute your dream, but the Storm can influence you to influence your dream to become a reality. There is no time to brag in the Storm.

In the Strom there is no comfort, if you think that the Storm can give you comfort. Actually the Storm is a test, trying you for where you want to be. The Storm doesn't care whether you cry or you feel sorry for yourself, your tears will never change the Storm, but the Storm can change your tears. Don't cry when you are in the Storm, they are many storms of life and they all need to be attacked by you. You cannot quit in the storm, if you quit the Storm will continue dragging you. Don't allow the storm to drag you, stand up and fight in the storm.

Those lighting are not real they want to scare you, don't run away, fight the Storm until you defeat the storm. The thunder's are not there for you. You need to walk by faith. In the storm it's a must for you to have faith and use it to fight. Faith is there to attack the Storm for you, for you cannot attack the storm physically.

Are you a young adult who is looking for a serious relationship but you don't find any, you are in the storm of not getting a relationship. Maybe you think that you are unattractive, the problem is that you don't know how to attack the storm you're facing. You are not aware that you are in a storm, because you only know about physical storms.

CHAPTER 9

You are in the Storm. Don't give up on your dream, your dream is to have a serious relationship with somebody who is also serious.

The reason why you are not getting a serious relationship is that you don't know what you want in a relationship, know what you want in a relationship, are you looking for money or are you looking for a lifetime relationship. Set your priorities of looking for a relationship straight. If you know what you want in a relationship you can have a serious relationship with somebody who is serious too. Fight the storm of being a failure in relationships, know what you want in a relationship. You are no longer a child, if you find yourself in a storm know that you have grown enough to fight the Storm, don't cry for help because nobody will hear you.

Be challenged by the storm to get what you want after the storm. Don't try to behave like you don't care when you are in the storm. Know why you are in a storm and what will happen when you don't fight the storm by using you faith. Fight until the storm itself bow down to you, don't be the one who bow down to the storm, make the storm bow down to you in the storm. If you can defeat the storm surely you can achieve that thing you are fighting for. Don't think about failing when you are in the storm, think about defeating the storm for a good course.

When you are in the storm don't allow the wind that blows to give you reason to give up. You might find yourself in the storm where people spread rumours about you. Don't allow what they spread about you discourage you or give you reason to run away from the storm, stand that storm of gossip. They will gossip and spread rumours about you for a moment. The more they gossip about you is the more they will strengthen you to attack the Storm, not because you want to prove them wrong, simply because you want to defeat, remember I said "the aim is not to prove anyone wrong but to complete what we started when nobody was there".

There are many storms in life that makes weak people manifest their weakness by running away from those storms. Are you going to flee the storm, because of what others do when they face the storm, don't run away, but face the storm.

Do u know why they rejected you before you can enter into the storm?
It's because they don't have the strength to stand the storm. You were able to stand the storm of rejection and you defeated it, so don't be afraid of any storm that comes your way, storm will always be there to test you. The real quality of a strong person is determined by the storms he or she faces in life. I know you are a mighty person you will not be afraid of the storm, if there were no storms in life, you were not going to know how stronger you are and you were not going to know the level of your faith. Storms are our playground ,is where you train your Faith ,if you do not experience storms will never know how to train his/her faith .

Sometimes people often say you are mad when you always say "I am okay" when you are in the storm. There are storms that does not need intervention of people because they might make things worse, people are not always there to give support they might be there aiming to make you fail fighting the storm. When they arrive the first thing that they do is to stop you from what you are doing ,e.g.

if they find you paying a bond house and you are struggling ,they will tell you that you should stop and you will stop, but they won't be there when you face the consequences .Where will you live when you stop paying rent? where will your children sleep? sometimes people make things to be more difficult that is why I say not every storm needs people who claim to can help when they make things to be worse. **Don't allow the storm to stop you from believing in your dream.**

In the storm there are false accusations that will arise from nowhere, you will be victimised for the things that you have never done, you will feel like you are not the right person to achieve the things that you want to achieve, false accusations has got the power to stress and make you doubt yourself. Being victimised does not mean that you can incomplete, people will try by all means to stop you from reaching your dreams, when they realise that they are left behind. The pain of victimisation is more painful, because your reputation might be ruined and your character will change to a bad one .

The only tool that can conquer victimisation is Faith and the object that can your pain of being falsely accused is forgiveness.

When people accuse you of the things that you have never done, don't hate them for there is no gain in hating, forgive them because forgiveness give birth to liberty. I remember when I was still a little boy, I was falsely accused of stealing money, I was not aware that I was in the Storm, but what I love about the storm that I encountered when I fifteen is that I managed to conquer it by forgiving people who falsely accused me even though they never came back to ask for forgiveness. There is power in forgiving people who falsely accuse you before they can come to ask for forgiveness. Indeed forgiveness is a sign of growth, if it wasn't for the storm that I experienced I wouldn't have become the person I am today. The aim of that storm was to distract me and lead me to jail, but because I managed to quickly forgive them it didn't happen. Don't be afraid of the Strom.

People who reject you now are aware of the storm that is coming ahead, the reason why they reject you is because they cannot stand against the Strom, they are giving you a chance to stand in the storm alone. Don't complain against them, they have done so to give you confidence to stand against the storm.

When the storm is over they will come back wanting to know whether you are still strong or the storm has destroyed you. Unfortunately they will find you stronger, than before they left you. People who reject you in the season of the storm are not meant to be part of your life, because they want you only when things are alright. Don't be intimidated by the Storm, it is there to test your faith. You attract dangerous storms, because you too are very dangerous, fact remains that you cannot attract what you don't relate with. **There is a victory in your storm.**

CHAPTER 10

Know Your Standard

Have your own principles. As a human being you must live life by your own principles, in order to fulfil your purpose by achieving your dream, if you don't have your own principles you will not be grounded, everything people might say can influence you easily, you will follow to the direction of the wind. Principles have the power to set good standard for you, you must live life based on your own principles.

What drives you, what gives you the meaning of life, are you just going to watch and never do anything to achieve it? If you have a goal of becoming a singer, you must Learn to listen to music that you want to sing, for you cannot listen to hip-hop if you want to sing Jazz, for what you entertain the most, becomes part of you. Are you aiming to be a billionaire, what are you going to do in order to become one? ,take a step.

Don't use evil strategies to become a billionaire, what you do must not be done on the dark side. Don't steal or kill people and sell their body parts in order to be a billionaire; you should have the desire of working hard in order to become a billionaire. Billionaires do not have to time to gossip and they don't entertain nonsense.

If you don't know your standard you will do whatever it is not good for your standard and also demote yourself to another standard which will decrease you to the standard you will never enjoy. Know who you are, know your purpose, know your dream, know what you want to do, know your goal, be the founder of your vision, take ownership of your dream. Don't be attracted to meretricious things.

Never try copy and paste what others are doing because your standard and theirs are not the same, you can copy and paste but never get the results they get when they do what they do, because you don't know what boost them to do what they are doing. Remember we are living in a generation whereby people love boosting their potentials.
The reason why they boost their potentials with foreign powers is that they don't believe in their own potentials and abilities.

Never boost your potentials and abilities by using foreign powers, because you are the one who is going to suffer at the end, know your standard. Always remember that anything that comes easy in your life is not going to be easy to maintain it. All you have to do is be patient and develop the spirit of patience, I know that it does take some time, don't rush. Don't feel insufficient when others are driving cars, getting married or marrying and buying houses, it's their season.

Your season is going to come and you will also enjoy your hard work. People who do not know what is hard work or hates hard work will always try to boost. Don't be fooled by those who are involved in occult and they are rich, for they are not gaining anything. Sweat for your dream, sweat for your purpose, sweat for your goal and sweat for what you want to have.

Don't make decisions based on what you see, but make decisions that will never take away your peace, if your peace can be taken away it's going to be easy for you to be involved in an organization that you hate the most. Protect your peace by doing what is right and by doing what will protect your Golden dream. Don't underestimate the ability you have when you come across those who have arrived in summer season when you are still in winter season.

Never imitate others, don't buy an umbrella when you are experiencing the winter season, simply because you see others holding umbrellas, you don't know their season, you may find that they are already in summer season. Knowing your standard helps you know what is best for your dream. When you know your standard, you will know where you are based. You cannot be based on business and produce the results of a Doctor. **Know where you are based and know your standard and know you are worthy. Be wise.**

Learn from an Eagle which does not contradict itself.
An Eagle have the ability to soar and fly, but birds can fly only. The moment you discover that you can be like an eagle it's when you realise that you doubted yourself for nothing. An eagle does not doubt itself, Eagle believes even when it sees an oncoming storm, for it knows that it can mount up to the higher altitude.

If an Eagle can consider to mount up in the midst of all birds, in order to posses its standard, who are you to be on the standard that doesn't belong to you, if you don't know your standard you will never know what belongs to you, you will always feel pity for yourself when things are taken away from you. know your standard.

Possess vitality, but for you to possess vitality you have to know your standard or set a standard for yourself, don't just be like anyone else, don't allow the wind to blow to east with you when you want to go to west. Don't reduce the effort you apply in your progress ,the moment you reduce that effort is when you will downgrade your standard to the standard of people who are stagnant. When we face some challenges we don't downgrade our standard ,we upgrade ourselves in order to make our dreams real. Don't allow those who downgraded their standards to encourage you to do the same.

Be tenacious. We are living in the environment where by people give up easily, if you allow the spirit that is affecting people in this environment to affect you too, it probably obvious that you will be like them by giving up in your dream. Don't give up on your dream, don't you know that the quality of patience is not determined by waiting but by having resolute attitude in everything you do .If you fail to be patient for your dream, surely you will fail to sustain your standard.

Be fearless; The real quality of knowing your standard is determined by how fearless you are. You cannot be fearless and be like others .The reason why an Eagle can soar is because its fearless, birds are afraid to soar because they are bound to be limited by their limitations, but they are not aware that they are limited ,their standard is limited. If your standard is limited then you are like birds .When you are fearless is easy for you not to be limited, you cannot be limited, when you are fearless expand your limits and become limitless in everything you do. You can be limitless and become the legend of your works, only if you are fearless.

If you find yourself being bound in limitation, then you were not born with qualities, if you were born with qualities you will not allow limitations to limit you, don't be limited like a fish, fish cannot do anything outside water or else it will die. The environment of the fish is water, you cannot take fish out of water and expect it to survive. But a fearless human being can be exposed to any environment and will be able to stand every challenge life may bring, life is full of challenges and most fearful people give up.
Be a fearless person who is ready to take a challenge and turn it into an opportunity, some people when faced with challenges they complain and end up blaming what they did before, because it has brought challenges to them.

Weak people always blame their past for the difficulties they experience, be a strong person with great actions. Do not associate yourself with great people, rather you should associate yourself with greater people in order to become great; when you associate yourself with great people they will despise and discourage you not to be on the same level with them. They will try to push you down because they know that you might surpass them and become greater.

If you want to cause great admiration you don't need to go around asking how to cause great admiration, you look for what makes you not cause great admiration and remove it in your life and start doing what will cause you to cause great admiration in the process of being associated with greater people, you cannot be associated with greater people and remain the same. Your attitudes changes when you starts walking into their steps.

The moment you start walking into the steps of greater people, your attitudes will change and your goals becomes adjusted ~Lethabokenedy.

CHAPTER 11

Know Your Mission

We are all born to accomplish what we are called for, but a lot of people forget what they were called for when they come across things of the world. Remember when you were born the world was like this, it had its own parts in every environment as today. Why keep on chasing the things that you found here on earth. Are you satisfied with what the world has, don't you want to be part of the world by accomplishing your mission here on earth?
Others have played their parts here on earth, you are the only one has not done so. Be creative, use your creativity to create what the society needs in order to benefit the seemingly dysfunctional environments, remember somebody contributed by putting efforts to make this world to be like what it is. I urge you to contribute with your dream towards building this beautiful world.

When you were born you found teachers in this world, they played their part to make you become who you are today. They imparted you with the knowledge that you were not born with, they raised you, they believed in you. Today you have a career or you still working towards having a career because of them. They gave you an idea of having a career; they took their time to teach you and feed you with knowledge that will help you for the rest of your life. But now because you are full of knowledge you don't want to share it with others who possess little knowledge. If you want to see that you can also play your part in this world, just reach your dream. The mission of your dream is not to make you rich, but to inspire others to fulfil their dreams.

The Aim Of Your Dream

Most people are now confused because they don't know the aim of their dreams, that is why it's easy for them to stop believing in their dreams. You cannot drink water if you don't know the aim of drinking water, you have to know the aim of drinking water in order to drink it, you cannot just drink water without a reason. You should know the aim of your dream. I remember the first time I went to Birchleigh North with my sister, my aim was to accompany her, so that she can do her assignments there. When I arrived, I was a little bit confused because it was my first time to be in a library. I was amazed by the books found in there.

Then I sat down and my sister said to me "Take one book from the shelves and read", I took a book and read it for about an hour, then I decided to put the book on the table. I said to myself "if this lady who wrote this book can write a book about her life, who am I not to write a book that could change somebody's life out there, I know people have dreams but they cannot reach them" then I developed the idea of writing this book, just after two month I started of. My aim while writing this book was to remind you about your dream. I believed in your dream the first day I started writing this book, I knew you needed this book to work on your dream. I wrote this book in order to activate your dream. I activated your dream, now is the time for you to activate somebody's dream by fulfilling your own dream.

Don't let nature nurture your dream, don't let what you see stop you from reaching the dream you have, if you fail to fulfil your dream, you have failed to accomplish your mission here on earth. Don't give up on your dream, I know it takes efforts and strength, but you will thank yourself someday.

Don't fail your dream. Your aim here on earth is to fulfil your dream. You will know that your dream is a servant to your purpose when you despise your dream, many people have given up on their dreams, because of not knowing the purpose of their dreams. If your aim is not to accomplish your call by reaching your dream then your aim is to reject the calling by accomplishing the things of the world.

Just because you failed before it does not mean that you cannot go far, sometimes we all encounter failure in life, nobody wants to fail. When you fail, it does not mean that you have to change the direction, if you don't encounter some challenges, then you are not on the right path, don't you know that challenges are the symptoms of greater dream.

You cannot have a greater dream without having the symptoms first. The smaller the symptoms the smaller the dream, the more the symptoms the bigger the dream. A woman cannot have a baby without experiencing the symptom called pregnancy.

Knowing your mission helps you to learn something in the season of having symptoms (challenges). The day you reject your dream that can accomplish your mission will be the day you reject your calling, remember we are all called, but it's up to us to fulfil the calling by accomplishing our missions. Nobody was born to be a spectator, we are all born to work hard and fulfil the calling. You may find that your mission is a doorway for your coming generation, if you fail to accomplish your mission, you will be failing your coming generation.

Don't be the reason why other people stop believing in their dreams, because there are young kids who look up to you, even today, you are their role model. Be a good role model, build their dreams by fulfilling yours first. Be a good example to them.

CHAPTER 11

There is a thin line between being lazy and hindering others to live their purposes, don't you know that your dream is a doorway, so that other people can discover theirs. If you don't do anything about your dream, there are many lives that will be affected, your failure will have negative impacts in many lives.

Now you may not realise that your dream is the head of many dreams, fulfil it, then you shall see that your dream has the greatest impact in many dreams, which are still wrapped for now. You have the power to unwrapped the wrapped dreams by reaching your dream first. Even though your dream might be difficult to achieve, you must achieve it.

CHAPTER 12

Maturity Matters

You cannot be matured without daily growth ~Lethabokenedy
Applying substantial effort will produce substantial results.

Gradual growth in your life will enhance your thinking capacity, growing gradually is the best thing ever. If you fail to grow on your daily basis then you cannot make progress over the period of time, because what makes progress in your life is your daily growth. Growing old is a common thing, but growing up is an individual thing, you cannot grow up if you fail to do something that will bring growth in your life. Sitting all days cannot help, but will help you reduce the level of your thinking capacity, the more you don't use your mind the more the things that are in your mind disappear gradually.

According to me, you might be physically constant but you cannot be mentally constant, it's up to you to reduce your positive thinking capacity or increase your thinking capacity by the effort you put in your dream. There should be continuous progress on your daily growth. The efforts that you should put toward your dream requires your thinking, the more you think the more you enhance your capacity, you cannot enhance your thinking capacity by talking alone, thinking increases your thinking capacity. There shouldn't be any limitations on your thinking capacity, you can think all the day, thinking positive things, but it's up to you to think positive or negative. If your mind can function continuously why don't you use it to think positively in order to do positive things. You cannot measure your maturity level if you fail to measure the level of your daily efforts, your daily efforts will display your maturity level.

You think before you can act or apply the effort, some of our dreams require a lot of thinking, that is necessary for us to think positive in order to do positive things.

Some people's dreams require a lot of labour, but you cannot labour without thinking, so in other words your mind plays an important role of being an engine of your daily efforts. Substantial efforts should be consistent. The substantial effort you put in today should be the substantial effort you're going to apply tomorrow. Those who fail are not failing, because their strategy is wrong, they fail simply because their daily efforts are not the same, they change their efforts, your effort should be the same in order to produce one thing.

If the efforts you put in differs, then even your results will differ, because variety of efforts cannot create one common thing, remember an effort is not an object or item that can be used for a certain function. We can use different objects to create a chair or table but we cannot use different efforts in building a dream, we will be diluting the dream in the process of building. They can use cement and a brick to build, but we cannot imitate them, because we only need similar efforts each and every day to create a beautiful Golden dream.

Do not ruin your dream by not being consistent with your everyday efforts. For you to produce your dream, you should apply substantial efforts that are similar. The reason why the mango tree does not produce the same amount of mangos every year, is because of the effort of water that is applied to them, in the drought season, the mango tree will produce less fruits, but if it's a rainy season the mango tree will produce many fruits. If the rain becomes consistent every year the mango tree will produce many mangos each year.

What Is Growth

Growth is the gradual increase of something that exists.
I believe you have heard many people talking about growth, maybe you don't understand what is growth. Let's say you have a business and you sell products, in order for you to make your business grow, you should upgrade the value of your products, so that your products can attract people who want to buy them. If you fail to upgrade the value of your products, then you've failed to grow your business. The more you update the value of your products the more you attract many customers to buy and the more they buy the more you make a good profit that leads to gradual growth.

Your dream needs your daily growth, which attracts maturity. It takes a matured person to realise that his dream is important, but it takes a fool to dilute his dream with negativity. The negativity may be allowing people to build your dream in your presence. A fool believes that you can trust all people with your dream, but the wise believes that you can only love them but never trust them with your dream, if they can hate you for nothing, what makes you believe that they can build your dream?

People whom you call your friends, do they need you when things are going well on their side or do they call you only when they need help from you.

This kinds of friends are parasite. Don't allow them to assess your dream when they are failing to handle their downfall, the reason they come to you looking for help is because they cannot handle their downfall and they believe that you can offer them the help they need, give them that help but don't trust them because in summer season they don't come to you they come to you only in winter season seeking for help.

Do they display the love they speak about towards you? No, they don't they are not your true friends, that is why maturity matters .When you are matured you will realise that they have made you their doctor, they only come to you when they are sick. When you are matured you will stop bringing dysfunctional people closer to you and you will stop fooling around with dysfunctional people.

Don't waste your effort trying to impress people who do not care about you, don't do things based on what people say, don't you know that phenomenal people do great work when there is not one to say congratulations. Don't do things simply because they are observing. Do great when there is no one who is watching, so that they cannot have the power to say "We know his struggle".

When you are matured you will know what you want, you will make sure you get what you want at the end of the day, you will work toward achieving what you want, you will not be lazy for it and you will work harder to achieve what you want. Most people have dreams but their dreams will remain as dreams, reason being they still have the mentality of kids, they are not aware that their mentality is killing them spiritually, actually they are committing spiritual suicide, for they are killing their dreams gradually. We as people need to change the way we think about our dreams, if we think like kids towards our goals or dreams, we will never reach them.
One has to be focused in order to focus on his own dreams, without focus it's not easy to believe in your dreams. Focus gives one an attitude that makes them to focus on their dreams and also focus attracts maturity. If we have the behaviour of kids which makes people lose focus and this behaviour, even brings about confusion, for they are adults who lacks maturity. People who still have childish behaviour will end up rejecting or neglecting their dreams. For that behaviour makes them believe that dreams are things to play with.

Many people are still in the process of maturity while a lot of people are not yet in the process of maturity. Those who are in the process of maturity try their best to match their words with their actions, but those who are not yet in the process of maturity, they act opposite to what they think of. It's your responsibility to grow and to be matured, the reason why some dreams are not reached is because people have the ability to dream but they don't have the ability to achieve or fulfil their dreams, they don't believe that they can fulfil their dreams, they only believe in dreaming. Dreaming big must be coupled with knowing how to reach or achieve what you have dreamt about when you were alone.

Some people depend on others, if others do not approve their dreams, then it's over with them. Don't stress on how you are going to fulfil your dream (Focus is the best weapon or tool to conquer fear). Being focused is what keeps you moving despite all the difficulties that life may bring on your road.

Difficulties determines the level of your maturity, you cannot face serious difficulties when you are not matured, you will face baby difficulties when you are not matured. When you are matured you will experience serious difficulties, reason being is that you attract things that are not dysfunctional, so they test the level of your maturity before they can work for you and if only you can deal with them you will be able to conquer even in the future. Do you know that people who are not matured always complain when they encounter problems in life they rush to look for help, do you think there's anyone who can help you fulfil your dreams while theirs are at the point of failure.

They will help you to reach failure not to conquer failure, be WISE (Not every tree becomes happy when the surrounding trees produces good fruits than itself).

Matured people do not complain, they seek solutions instead of looking for helpers who will end up being problems to them. Mature people do not bother themselves by seeking approval or solutions from others, because they know that they carry solutions within them.

Solution is not what you look for, but it's what you create, creating solution gives you access to solve problems, you cannot solve a problem with a solution that you don't have. Create solutions, don't look for solutions, we are all given the ability to create whatever we could desire to create (in the beginning there was no electricity, but somebody came with an idea of creating electricity, then he created electricity, I believe that there were some people who were not approving his vision, but he didn't allow them to discourage him. I believe that "they said he is crazy, he is imagining things that do not exist". But today we have got electricity because of him, this is all because of Maturity, he was matured that is why he was able to fulfil his dream). Lacking maturity is what makes people fail in life.

In life there are certain things that makes people lose concentration, people tend to say I WANT TO PROVE THEM WRONG, in life we don't prove anyone wrong, we have to understand that some people's minds are paralyzed that is why they say negative things concerning our lives. Don't use anger as motivation to achieve a particular goal, anger can terminate you from your destiny or race, learn to control yourself. You don't need to prove anyone wrong or compete with anyone, you can only compete with your positive thoughts. Maturity is what makes your dream a reality.

The game has already begun you are the one who can determine the outcome, remember the aim of your game is to get a reward, because reward is better than a prize.

Compete with your positive thoughts by making them realities. Be great and allow your greatness become a ladder for others, specially those who do not believe they can fulfil their dreams.

"Don't allow your weakness undermine your greatness"

A wise man will hear and will increase learning and a man of understanding shall attain unto wise counsels (Proverbs 1:5). What are you learning when you are with your friends?
What makes you to increase what you are learning? You cannot be proud of learning about hatred, it's an abomination for a person like you to learn about hatred when you are with your friends, it's either you separate yourself with your friends who makes you to learn about hatred for the sake of your Genuine dream or you stay with them for the dilution of your dream with negativity, it's your choice to choose them or your dream.

For your dream to become genuine you must learn meaningful things not negative things, if you are a parent how can you allow your child to learn how to sleep with men instead of learning how to study, you are diluting the dream of your child with negativity, tomorrow you're going to blame your child for sleeping with men outside. If you are a young man how can you be proud of sleeping with many women. You cannot achieve your goals or fulfil your dreams with such habits, you need to separate yourself from them, before it's too late.

My sister having many boyfriends in the name of money is not taking you anywhere, you must learn to stand on your own. I believe you have a genuine dream, so why don't you stop doing those foolishness things and start building your dream today, if I were you I was going to take my phone right now and start deleting contacts of people who are wasting my time. You cannot reach your Genuine Dream by associating with time consumers.

Never fail your parents, for they believed in you. The day your mother conceived you she believed in you for greater things.

Learn meaningful things, if you want to become a role model to somebody, learning is a way of acquiring skills by practicing; what are you practicing? In order to fulfil your dream, you have to learn what will build your dream and not what will corrupt the foundation of your dream. A corrupted foundation cannot be change by the structure of the building, no matter how beautiful the structure is, the only way to incorrupt the foundation is to demolish it, while there is still time. Don't build your dream on a corruptible foundation. This will help you not waste time and change as you move forward.

The reason why others start to change along the way when they are trying to build their dreams, is because they allowed the negativity to corrupt the foundation of their dreams and the body of their dreams is also suffering, because they are still learning things that corrupt people's minds. There are some things that will enjoy when you are learning them but they are too dangerous for your dream, they can drain your faculty.

Conclusion of being mature, there is a remedy that you can bring into your dream. There are some people in this life that will try to test the level of your maturity, by spreading negative things about you, what you can do to avoid this situation is keep quiet and act as if nothing is happening, don't react because your reaction might cause irreparable damages in your dream. Anyone who allows the wind to blow with him he's like an empty tin that makes a lot of noise and disturbs many. Don't bring tins near you, bring people who have occupations or who are working towards having an occupations in life. If you bring tins near you they will upgrade the level of your fear and downgrade the demission of your faith.

If you bring tins near you they will beneath you, what is that you are going to do when a tin is making lot of noise near you? The aim of a tin is to make a noise that will disturb those who are busy with meaningful things. A tin has the ability to catch your attention even thought it's small and useless, remember useless objects want all the useful objects to be like them, reason being that they are already used, they want other useful and unused objects to share the same room with them. Look around you and discover the tins that disturbs you when you try to be committed to your dream. Repel away from any tin that makes a lot of noise for you.

CHAPTER 13

Be Intentional

The dream of the frog was to have an active stream. The frog arrived at the stream which seemed to be dysfunctional, the frog started digging the stream in order to prepare for it.
The frog realised that the stream needs attention, reason being is that **"everything that is not taken care of, becomes diluted or contaminated with negativity"**. The frog shaped the stream and made it look beautiful than before.

When the frog was busy polishing the neglected stream, it happened that water started to spring up from the ground. The frog was not surprised, it was filled with Joy within, because its dream was being fulfilled, even if it took time to come to pass.
The frog realised that there is no dream that one cannot achieve, but one needs preparation, persistent, perseverance, hope, endurance and a resolute mind, which attract a resolute attitude.

Giving birth to a dream is not easy, you can be pregnant with a dream, but it requires you to have a resolute attitude to give birth to a best dream you are pregnant with.

The only thing which differentiate failures and achievers is the effort they put in building their dreams. I believe that the efforts that we put in daily towards making a progress will differentiate us at the end.
If you have three seeds and I also have three seeds, what will differentiate us is how we plant or sow them. You can sow one and I may sow all the three, but it does not mean that you will reap the same thing as I will, you will reap from one seed and I will reap from the three seeds. Our harvests will not be the same.

Putting in efforts to your daily progress towards reaching your dream is like sowing a seed hoping to enjoy the fruits of the seed later. e.g. if you want to become the best driver, you should practice driving everyday by driving in a good way.

When you want to be a good singer you should practice singing by singing, make sure you practice singing using the songs that you know and understand.

Don't try to be somebody else, be you and do what you are capable of doing, they are many people who hide their true capabilities, by trying to be what they are not. Pretenders cannot reach a genuine dream, they can fake a dream as they are faking their true character. How can you fake your character and expect to achieve a genuine dream. If you are failing to be real you then forget about reaching a real dream. Don't hide your true abilities and character if you want to reach your dream.

What Are You Pregnant With?

Whatever you are pregnant with, will surely be birthed, some are pregnant with failure, because they have been impregnated by the sperm which is called fear. Don't you know that fear is a dangerous sperm that can impregnate one and cause one to give birth to failure.

Many who fail, they are not failing because they lack abilities, it's simply because they allowed fear to impregnate them when they started, but failure is a lesson that teaches one to stop allowing fear to impregnate him or her when building a dream. Pregnancy is a matter of substance, you have to be pregnant with something that is important, don't just be pregnant without knowing the purpose of being pregnant.

When a woman is pregnant there are some foods that she is not allowed to eat, because they will affect the unborn child. Some are pregnant with positivity but they still associate themselves with negative people, the people you associate yourself with will affect the one who is within you. Do not go to places that are not good for your pregnancy, how can you be pregnant and still drink alcohol, how can you have a dream and still associate yourself with people who lack dreams for their lives.

A pregnant woman expose herself to environment like clinics for check ups, so you have a dream and you know that your dream is related to books, why don't you go to library and read the books that will accelerate your dream. Make sure that all the environments you expose yourself to contribute to your dream. If you don't expose yourself to environment that will provoke your dream, then you are giving failure a chance in your life by being exposed to wrong environments.

Don't be pregnant with something that will dilute your dream or waste your time. Be pregnant with positivity, then you will give birth to your dream and don't rush to give birth wait for the right time to give birth, don't run away from the process that will create labour pains, because you can't give birth if you don't experience labour pains.

People can fake pregnancies, but the day to give birth is coming, what you are faking will shame you when others are giving birth to real babies. Don't waste time trying to fake your dream, people pretend to be pregnant with something that they know they are not pregnant with. If you are okay in your head you will never fake your dream, but if you are not okay in your head you can fake your dream aiming to please.

If you are going to allow stop signs (hazards of life) to stop you then you are going to consume the time that was meant to build up your dream. A tree does not stop producing fruits, it changes its habit in order to produce good fruits. The tree does not change the roots but it changes its leaves so that it can produce good fruits. If you going to change your direction, because of hazards of life then you will be failing your dream.

I believe that this piece of writing has change you, there is nothing that you cannot achieve, all you have to do is to follow the process and never say it's too late. If you think your enthusiasm is not sufficient for your dream then generate your enthusiasm by associating yourself with people who are already living the dream you want to achieve.
If you have failed before don't call yourself a failure, you are not a failure, failure is just a word and remember that you have learned your lesson .Go and reach that Golden dream you have. Change the strategy that made you fail, don't' change your dream. If you can dream it then you achieve it and live it.

CHAPTER 13

You are a manufacturer of your dream, the pillar of your dream, the achiever of your dream and that genuine dream is yours.

Defects are caused by a lack of commitment, commitment prevents defects ~ Lethabokenedy

Be Like An Eagle

For an Eagle to get fish it does not wait for the fish to come out of the water, rather the eagle goes down in the water to get a fish, the act is risky and dangerous, but the Eagle is not afraid of the danger of water. If the dream of an Eagle is to eat a fish, it does not change its dream because of the environment that the fish lives in, but it strategize how it's going to get the fish out of the water, the Eagle does not allow the environment of the fish to terrify it.

The Eagle have strong vision, it can identify its prey until it get it, because an Eagle is attentive, it does not do something without planning. The eyes of an Eagle are specially designed for a long distance focus and clarity. Spot your dream the way an Eagle stop its prey. Your dream is your prey, if you don't become a predator of your dream, then your dream will not be your prey. An Eagle has the ability to lift a goat up, this means that the Eagle does not allow the weight of the goat stopping it from eating goat meat. If your dream is harder to achieve it means that your dream is greater, for the harder the dream to reach the bigger the dream.

Don't change your dream, because of the environment of your dream, go take your dream in that environment, but first have a strategy. Observe and see what makes others fail to achieve the dream you have, before going for it and if you spot what makes others fail, then you will never fail because you going to avoid what makes them fail, if it's a lack commitment, you're going to commit yourself to your dream.

Defects are the effects of lack of commitment. Your dream gives you genuine power to live it and reach it. Go reach your dream, stop fooling around with negative people.

The reason why an Eagle does not associate itself with birds is that birds can downgrade the value of the Eagle, don't associate yourself with anyone who can reduce your value. The Eagle knows its value, hence it does not eat dead meat. There are some times in life where by you can end up eating dead meat simply, because you are walking with the wrong crowd. Don't be associated with the crowd which eats anything when they are hungry. Walk with people who can add value in your life, not to downgrade your value. You are responsible for your dream, I believe that one day we will meet and you will give me a feedback about how this piece of writing has change your life and how it helped you to fulfil your dream. I love you and I believe in your dream, I believe you can bring the change in your life and in your community through this piece of writing. I call this book a piece of writing.

CONSIDER THE FOLLOWING

Success Requires Maintenance

Most people who are successful today know how to maintain their success, reason why their success becomes exceptional success. If you are going to be successful, you are supposed to continue paying attention to the efforts you put in towards your dream. People who have temporary success are those who think that they have already arrived, they don't know that there are dimensions of success. Coca cola company does not stop selling cokes when they have sold all the cokes that they have produced, they continue producing more cokes in order to maintain their success.

Success is like a chain cycle, it does not reach the level where by one has to stop working hard, the more you become successful the more your success requires a lot of your time. Those who stop paying attention to their success when they have tasted the sugar of success will never taste the honey of success. If you continue maintaining your success, you will taste the honey of success.

Have An Initial Strategy

The initial stage of building a house is a foundation. Without the foundation we cannot guarantee the quality of the building, foundations gives us the guarantee that the building will last longer. If you have a massive dream, you must have an initial dream that will take you to your massive dream, e.g. a business person does not start by advertising his or her business, there is something that is called business profile or business proposal, these are foundations of a business.

These are the initial stages of a business according to me. Having an initial dream for your massive dream will help you know why you are willing to reach that dream. A student who want to become a Doctor does not become a Doctor automatically, he or she has to study in order to become a doctor, the process of studying is the initial stage of becoming a doctor. Planning is a way of showing that you have a plan, you cannot plan if you don't have a plan.

CONSIDER THE FOLLOWING

Ignore The Haters

Ask God for guidance in the journey of fulfilling your dream, always pray to God. Sometimes people hate you simply because you are dreaming more than they are, and that not your problem. We are all given brains to think and dream, but they are using their brains to do things that will never reward them. We are given freedom of choice. If you know very well that people are your enemies don't fight them, leave them to God. Haters are there to distract you, don't allow them to distract you. Leave them to God, let God tackle them, don't tackle them because you might get hurt in the process of dealing with them. If you pay attention to fighting with your enemies, it means that your dream is not a necessity to you.

Don't Stop

You have been crawling for a long time; now is time to stand up and walk. A baby doesn't need to be taught how to walk, but a baby takes a big decision of walking without permission of the parents. Every baby who is crawling always tries to stand up and walk and when the baby falls ,he or she do not stop what she or he is doing . If we can learn the consistency that babies have we can go far in life, their consistency is something that keeps pushing them to try to stand up and walk.

When a baby sees others walking, the baby doesn't sit down or continuing crawling, the baby tries to be like them, it does not mean the baby is imitating others, the baby sees walking a necessity not an imitation activity. What makes a baby not to give up is patience, their patience helps them to repel from anger, we as old people always have anger, when things are not going according to our plan, we get angry.

The more we become angry the more we repel from patience, anger and patience cannot share the same room together. Be consistent like a baby who tries to walks and be patient in everything you do. Patience is the key that keeps one in the Game.

Have A Revelation

When you have a revelation, self-development becomes activated automatically. Self-development is an individual thing that comes through revelation, when you have a revelation about your dream, you will realise that it a must for you to develop yourself. Self development helps you to know the definition of your dream. Never copy others methods in the process of developing yourself, self development organise you to be organised about your dream. Self development is being able to know why you are you? Knowing whom you are helps you to know why you should maintain what you are about to achieve, if you don't know who you are, you will not see the need to maintain your dream.

Self development is knowing in which category you fall under in life, we have got exceptional, average and normal people. What is your category, does your category satisfy you? If you want to be exceptional, you should try exceptional things in the process of self development. Don't pull back, forward is favoured than backward.

Revival Of The Winner

When Patience takes over, impatience disappears,
When impatience disappears the soul gets revival.
Nothing can beneath the soul that carries patience, for patience
gives hope to the soul. Patience uplift the human spirit in tough
times. Enthusiasm is the first born of patience, for patience gives
the human spirit the ability to develop enthusiasm for a specific
Dream in tough times.

The source of blissful life is to endure hard times .
Every soul that endures hard times will enjoy the fruits of hard
times. Hard times shape a character. Hard times prove a genuine
character, for it test the Patience of the character, for Patience is
the aspect of a character. A soul that has a good
Character, has a genuine patience.

Every winner in this universe
has experienced hard times and conquered hard times, for what
makes a winner is conquering hard times by using magnetism tool
which is patience that attract phenomenal habits in hard times.
When patience takes over, impatience disappears.
Patience of a winner is tested by hard times.

Consider This

Ask guidance from God
Don't blame people for your failure
Don't bring dysfunctional people closer to you
Don't beg people to go your direction
Repel from negativity and don't allow people to exploit you
Do the common in an uncommon way
Don't fake what you do ,let is be genuine
Learn to be resourceful
Learn to be different
Don't allow reality to stop you from achieving your dreams
Don't allow people to discourage you
Don't have disorder of priorities
Use your skills for good course
Have vivid vision
Be patient its going to take some time
Never entertain excuses
Work harder when your season arrives
Avoid being haughty
Don't let their season to intimidate your season
The aim is not to compete but to complete
Desire to finish what you start
Dream to accomplish your dream
Desire to have achievements in life
You cannot become great when you are not willing to humble
yourself, Humble yourself in order to become Great

~Lethabokenedy